Wilbur Marvin Carpenter

The Self-Instructor's Manual of Short-Hand

A labor-saving adaptation of the Isaac Pitman phonography, conducting

the student into the reporting style at the outset.

Wilbur Marvin Carpenter

The Self-Instructor's Manual of Short-Hand
A labor-saving adaptation of the Isaac Pitman phonography, conducting the student into the reporting style at the outset.

ISBN/EAN: 9783337311810

Printed in Europe, USA, Canada, Australia, Japan

Cover: Foto ©Paul-Georg Meister /pixelio.de

More available books at **www.hansebooks.com**

THE

SELF-INSTRUCTOR'S

MANUAL OF SHORT-HAND.

A LABOR-SAVING ADAPTATION OF THE ISAAC PITMAN PHONOGRAPHY,

CONDUCTING THE STUDENT

Into the Reporting Style at the Outset.

AS TAUGHT IN THE

BRYANT & STRATTON BUSINESS and SHORT-HAND SCHOOL

SAINT LOUIS, MO.

—BY—

THOS. M. ROGERS AND W. M. CARPENTER.

PUBLISHED FOR W. M. CARPENTER.

ST. LOUIS:
RIVERSIDE PRINTING HOUSE, 302 N. MAIN STREET.
1885.

PREFACE.

This work although small is the result of long study and observation, and a careful study of its pages will lead to the acquisition of the Reporting Style of Short-hand in as short a time as is generally required to master the Corresponding Style. While in a condensed form, every principle is presented and nothing which would aid the student has been omitted. The original intention was to issue only a small pamphlet advocating and explaining a method of teaching the Reporting Style from the outset by means of writing exercises, consisting of monosyllables and short words in ordinary use, and the reduction of the usual large list of "grammalogues," first suggested and put into actual practice years ago by Dr. W. M. Carpenter, proprietor of the Bryant & Stratton College, St. Louis, and a copyright was secured in 1884. However, in the course of teaching, various other improvements, among which were a simple aid in memorizing the consonants, the grouping of the vowel sounds in their proper position with reference to the line of writing, and comprehensive illustrated rules for writing outlines in position, rules for the use of the stroke or contracted W, phrase writing at the outset, method of writing the combination *s* and *r*, the proper employment of the *l* and *r* hooks, method of representing the combination *s*, *t* and *r*, *s*, *t* and *f*, *s*, *t* and *v*, and *s*, *t* and *n*, when to use the *f* or *v* hook in the middle of words, the proper use of the *ter* hook, what half-length stems should not be joined, a sign for the combination *r* and *m*, when to use the stroke MP-B, considering all words either primitive or derivative, a list of "regular prefixes," which enables the student to write any word with but little if any hesitation, rules for forming contractions, expression of initials, method of acquiring speed, list of words taking the *l* or *r* hooks, the simplification of the various rules and principles, and reading exercises consisting of monosyllables, words in ordinary use and those which generally prove troublesome to the student, all unvocalized and written in the proper position, were introduced by Thos. M. Rogers, the instructor, and it was finally decided to issue a complete manual, differing from all others heretofore published in that the science of Short-hand can easily be learned from it without the aid of a teacher. In accordance with this idea, everything that puzzled the student was noted, every principle that appeared difficult to understand was carefully studied to find the best method of simplifying it, rules were written and rewritten, and nothing was left undone which would in any manner lessen the labor of the student. When the lessons were so arranged, by the instructor, that the student without hard study could in a week or ten days begin dictation practice with an excellent understanding of the Reporting Style of Short-hand, preparations were made for the publication of the Manual. Few text books contain more useful engraved Short-hand, and none such valuable and systematically arranged writing exercises with sentences keyed so that the student knows whether or not to take advantage of any preceding shortening methods.

The "Corresponding Style" has been ignored, because it accustoms the student to a disconnected and lengthy style of writing wholly incompatible with rapid work, which it is necessary to unlearn before proficiency in the Reporting Style can be acquired. The Reporting Style is taken up at the beginning, and the exercises are so arranged that no word is given the student to write until all the principles contained in the proper formation of the outline have been presented; hence there can be no hesitancy in writing the word in actual reporting, because but one outline has ever been used to express it. By discarding the "Corresponding Style" much time has been saved the student which can be employed to excellent advantage in practicing from dictation, and a speed of from eighty to one hundred words a minute attained in less than one-half the time required by the old method of instruction.

The most noticeable feature, however, is the absence of a large list of "grammalogues" or "word signs," thus saving the student a vast amount of hard study. The word signs given are suggestive of the words of which they are symbols, and the task of memorizing them is thus materially lessened. This reduction is made by the employment of various shortening principles and the application of a few rules compiled expressly for this work. Over three-fourths of the "grammalogues," given in Pitman's "Reporter's Companion" to be memorized are only the skeletons of the words, are not arbitrary or contracted in any manner, but are simply the outlines of the words written in the regular Reporting Style. Had the Reporting Style been taught from the beginning there would have been no necessity for putting these words in a list and calling them "grammalogues" and much valuable time consumed in this memorization could be saved and better employed in writing from dictation.

The rules for the formation of contractions will be found of great value, and their employment will do away with the necessity of burdening the memory with a large list of contracted outlines, as words can be legibly contracted at will and without hesitation. The rules are the result of careful observation and experiment.

The consonant stems are those given in Pitman's "Ninth" Edition of Phonography, and admit of no improvement. They furnish better Phonographic material than those of his last, or "Tenth" Edition, and having stood the test of time stand upon their merits. The various modifications are those suggested by the leading American reporters—ones that have stood the severe test of actual verbatim reporting—and have been introduced into the work for the purpose of giving the student a Short-hand containing not only Isaac Pitman's ideas, but also those of others, and one that is legible, rapid, easy of acquisition and founded upon the best.

THE AUTHORS.

ADVICE TO STUDENTS.

Phonography should *always* be written on single ruled paper, with about half-an-inch space between the lines. The pen or pencil should be held between the first and second fingers, and be kept in place by a gentle pressure of the thumb.

The characters must be made correctly, of proper *slope, length* and *shade,* instead of hurriedly; speed comes by practice. Simple curved stems must have no hooks or flourishes at the ends, and perpendicular stems must not lean to the right.

The consonants should be about one-sixth of an inch in length,—not more under any consideration, until the lengthening principle is reached. A habit easy to contract but difficult to dispose of is that of writing the outlines too long, and should be avoided if the student wishes to succeed as a reporter. Long outlines retard speed, and have to be made hurriedly and therefore less accurately than though the stems were shorter. In rapidly writing the hand naturally travels over more space than when writing slowly, and if the student permits himself or is permitted to write large while learning the theory and receiving his first dictation exercise, he will find himself handicapped when he tries to increase his speed, and will either have to form a new style of writing, or never reach the goal of his ambition. Should any one who may be studying some other system, say your characters are too small, do not relinquish them and you will soon be able to convince your advisor that he, not you, has been writing incorrectly. Heavy curved stems should be thickest at the top and taper towards the bottom.

Writing exercises should be written again and again until a speed of not less than forty words a minute is acquired; by so doing the outlines of the different words become so fixed in the mind, that there will be no hesitation at any time in writing them; and the student begins dictation practice with a "vocabulary" of between five hundred and six hundred words of frequent occurrence, which will be of more value than any list of "grammalogues" that could be compiled, besides having the principles of their formation thoroughly at his command. Whatever the student writes must be read and re-read until there is no hesitation in the transcribing, and this reading aids to a remarkable extent the facility of writing. The fact must be borne in mind: No matter how rapidly we write if we cannot transcribe our notes, they are worse than useless.

The student must impress upon his mind the fact that Phonography is writing by sound and not according to the ordinary spelling. Thus the word *though* as commonly spelled is pronounced as though spelled *tho*, and is so written in Short-hand; *neigh, knee, know, sioux, view, burough, age, match, wreath, wreathe,* would be written, *na, ne, no, su, vu, burō, aj, mach, rēth, rēdh.* N before K has the sound of NG, and *bank* should be written as though spelled *bangk.* The Roman letter C has no equivalent sign in Phonography, as it has at times the sound of *k, s* and *sh,* as in the words *cat, ace, commercial,* which in Phonography would be written as though spelled, *kat, ās, komershal.* Q and X also have no corresponding sign in Phonography, their sounds being *kw, eks* and *egz,* they are so represented; thus, *quail* would be written *kwal; extra, ekstra; exact, egzakt; exaggerate, egzajrāt; exhaust, egzawst.*

Become perfectly familiar with one lesson before attempting another.

Carefully review each day the lesson of the previous one. This helps the memory, and impresses all the points more clearly in the mind.

Read everything you write, and spend as much time in reading your notes as you do in writing. A non-observance of this rule will cause infinite trouble in the student's first attempts at reporting.

§ 1. SIMPLE CONSONANT STEMS.

TABLE OF CONSONANTS.

＼ Pe	＼ Be	│ Te	│ De	／ CHay	／ Jay
— Kay	— Gay	＼ eF	＼ Ve	（ tTH	（ DHe
) eS	) Ze	／ tSH	／ ZHe	⌐ eL	＼ eR
⌢ eM	⌣ eN	⌣ tNG	＼ Way	⌐ Yay	⌢ eMP-B
∕ Hay	⌢ wL	∪ wR	⌢ wM	⌣ wN	∕ Ree

§ 2. By referring to the foregoing table it will be seen that B is a heavy P, D a heavy T, J a heavy CH, G a heavy K, V a heavy F, DH a heavy TH, Z a heavy S, ZH a heavy SH, W a heavy R, Y a heavy L, MP a heavy M, and NG a heavy N. Another peculiarity is that the light consonant sounds are represented by corresponding light signs, and heavy sounds by heavy signs. L and R joined form an arch, and F and SH joined form an inverted one, while the four could be so joined as to form a complete circle. A circle divided by lines written through it in the direction of P and CH would form TH, S, M and N. N and M with small initial hooks become wN and wM, and L and Ree with large initial hooks become wL and wR. Ree is written at an angle half-way between K and CH. J is used to represent the soft sound of G in such words as *George, germ, age,* etc., and G the hard sounds in *gay, get, gate,* etc. TH is used in words having the sound of *th* in *breath,* and DH in words having the sounds of *the* in *breathe,* and *th* in *they.*

§ 3. Perpendicular, inclined and heavy strokes are always written downward.

§ 4. Horizontal strokes are written from left to right.

§ 5. When standing alone SH is always written *downward* and L upward. The straight stem Ree is *always* written *upward.*

§ 6. When standing alone CH and Ree are distinguished by a difference of slope, CH being written at an inclination of sixty degrees from the horizontal, and Ree thirty. When joined to other stems they are distinguished by difference of stroke, CH *always* being written *downward* and Ree *upward;* thus, ⌐ *chap,* ／ *rap.*

VOWELS AND DIPHTHONGS.

¿ 7. There are twelve distinct vowel sounds, six long and six short. Three of the six long vowels are indicated by a heavy dash and three by a heavy dot, written at the beginning, middle and end of a consonant. Three of the short vowels are indicated by a light dash and three by a light dot, written in the same positions as the long.

¿ 8. The following scale will show the signs for and positions of the vowels:

LONG DOT VOWELS.		LONG DASH VOWELS.	
First place	a as in calm		a as in bali
Second "	a as in fade		o as in lode
Third "	ea as in peal		oo as in food

SHORT DOT VOWELS.		SHORT DASH VOWELS.	
First place	a as in bat		o as in on
Second "	e as in bet		u as in up
Third "	i as in pit		oo as in foot

¿ 9. The double vowel sounds heard in the words *ice, owl, boy,* are represented by small angular marks, and *iew* as in *view,* by a small curve, written to the consonant like a simple sign. *Three* occupy the *first,* and *one* the *third* position, as shown by the following:

TABLE OF DIPHTHONGS.

I   *ai* as in *aisle* and *i* in *ice.*

OI   *oy* as in *boy* and *oi* in *coil.*

OW   *ow* as in *cow* and *ough* in *bough.*

EW   *iew* as in *view* and *ue* in *due.*

¿ 10. In inserting a vowel that comes before a consonant it is written to the *left* of the stem if upright or inclined, and *above* if horizontal. When a vowel comes after a consonant it is written to the *right* of the stem if perpendicular or inclined, and *below* if horizontal. A vowel written at the left of a perpendicular or inclined stem, or above a horizontal, is read first; written at the right of a perpendicular or inclined stem, or below a horizontal, it is read after the stem.

§ 11. A dash vowel should be written at a right angle with the consonant stem, but should *not* be allowed to touch.

§ 12. The signs for the diphthongs are never inclined to correspond with the direction of the consonant stem to which they are written; but when convenient, inital *I* and final *iew* may be joined to the consonant.

§ 13. The different sounds of the vowels and diphthongs must be learned so that when a word is pronounced there will be no hesitation in determining the character and sounds of the vowel or vowels contained in it, and when facility in distinguishing the various sounds is acquired and the position readily determined, the insertion of vowels may cease and only the outline of the word "written in position," need be employed. The object of memorizing the different signs, representing the different vowel signs and their three positions, is simply to associate the sound with its proper position in reference to the line of writing, so that the first perpendicular or inclined, or only stem in the word, may be written *above, on* or *through* the line, or if a horizontal stem, *above, on* or *just below* the line. If the proper sound of the accented or only vowel in the word can be determined, then the writing of the *outline* or consonants in position becomes an easy task, for the *first* perpendicular or inclined stem is written in the position of its accented vowel, whether a vowel, the sound of which is *first, second* or *third* place. In actual reporting the vowels are very rarely used, and yet the notes are just as legible as though fully vocalized. This being the case then it will not be necessary to insert the vowel signs in early writing providing, however, the outline is written in its proper position. "But how are we to know what the characters represent if no vowels are written," some one asks, "the stroke T means an initial and also would stand for *tea*, and how are we to know which is meant?" The *context*, or that which precedes and follows the T would determine, the same as in ordinary conversation, when we hear the sound of T we know what it means simply by what has been said before and is said after it. In certain cases, in words like *Idea, iota,* where there are two or more vowels and only one consonant stem, then it should be partly vocalized, the diphthong *i* at least being inserted.

§ 14. Each of the consonant stems are written in three positions, corresponding with the three vowel positions, and like them called first, second and third.

§ 14a. The *first* thing the student should do before beginning to write words is to thoroughly memorize the different vowel sounds and their relative position as regards the line of writing *i. e*—the ruled lines across the page of the reporting book or paper. As it is unnecessary to vocalize in actual reporting. except when writing proper names, technical, or words of infrequent occurrence, the student need not insert any vowels. To enable the student to easily memorize the different vowel sounds and the proper position of each, the following tables have been arranged, together with simple, comprehensive and illustrated rules for writing the outlines of words in position as they would be in actual reporting. If these tables and rules are so memorized that when a word is spoken or read the position of its *accented* or *only* vowel is readily determined, the student has mastered the hardest part of his work. Always bear in mind that you spell by sound and *not* according to any dictionary; for instance the verb *bow* and noun *bough*, although differing in ordinary spelling, yet in Phonography the sounds being the same, *ow* as in *cow*, they would be written alike, by the stem P in the *first* position. Final W and Y are *not* consonants, therefore should *not* be written as such; "y" sometimes has the sound of *i* as in *it*, as in *pity*, the sound of *i* in *ice*, as *by*, and sometimes in connection with a vowel forms a diphthong with the sound of *i* or *a*, as in *buy* and *bay;* "w" sometimes occurs in connection with a vowel and forms a diphthong, as in *cow*, or following an *o*, having the same sound of the *o* in *poke*, is not sounded at all, as in *low*, which is written by the stem L in the *second* position. When "e" is the last letter in a word it denotes that the preceding vowel is long.

VOWEL SOUNDS AND RULES FOR POSITION WRITING.

§ 15. FIRST POSITION SOUNDS.

a as in *calm*,	*aw* as in *awl*,	*o* as in *on*
i as in *ice*,	*oy* as in *boy*,	*ow* as in *cow*,
a as in *at*.		

In writing words of one consonant, if the *accented* or *only* vowel has any one of the preceding sounds, the stem, if *perpendicular* or *inclined*, must be so written that the *lower* end will be about *one-half* the *height* of a T above the line of writing, but if the stem is *horizontal* it should be written about *one-sixth* of inch or the height of a T above the line. If there are two or more consonants in a word whose *accented* or *only* vowel has any one of the "First Position Sounds" the FIRST *perpendicular or inclined* stem must be written *above* the line the same as if it were the only consonant in the word, and the other consonant or consonants joined to it without lifting the pencil from the paper; but if the consonant stems are *all* horizontal, write them about one-sixth of an inch above the line.

Write in accordance with preceding rule, omitting the vowels and *all* consonants *not* sounded:

Pa	ma	annoy	cow	thaw	maw	back
pie	by	pack	buy	palm	odd	chap
at	add	dye	lie	law	chop	shop

₹ 16. SECOND POSITION SOUNDS.

a as in *make*,   *o* as in *poke*,   *u* as in *up*,

e as in *peck*,   *a* as in *air*,   *a* as in *pare*.

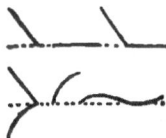

In writing words of one consonant, if the *accented* or *only* vowel has any one of the preceding sounds, the stem, if *perpendicular* or *inclined*, must be so written that the *lower end* of down-strokes and the *beginning* of up-strokes will *rest* upon the line. If there are two or more consonants in a word whose *accented* or *only* vowel has any one of the "Second Position Sounds" the FIRST *perpendicular* or *inclined stem* must be so written that it will *rest* upon the line the same as if it were the only consonant in the word, and the other consonant or consonants joined to it, without lifting the pencil from the paper; but if the consonant stems are *all* horizontal write them upon the line.

Write in accordance with preceding rule, omitting the vowels and *all* consonants *not* sounded:

Pay	oat	owed	know	fair	peck	share
may	ate	low	beau	bake	led	poke
lay	air	mow	show	both	edge	muck

THIRD POSITION SOUNDS.

ea as in *eat*,   *i* as in *it*,   *oo* as in *took*,

oo as in *boom*,   *iew* as in *view*,   *ee* as in *eel*.

In writing words of one consonant, if the *accented* or *only* vowel has any one of the preceding sounds, the stem, if *perpendicular* or *inclined*, must be so written that it will be *divided* by the line of writing into two equal parts, but if the stem is horizontal write it *just below* the line. If there are two or more consonants in a word whose *accented* or *only* vowel has any one of the "Third Position Sounds" the FIRST *perpendicular* or *inclined* stem must be written *through* the line the same as if it were the only consonant in the word, and the other consonant or consonants joined to it without lifting the pencil from the paper; but if the consonant stems are *all* horizontal write them just below the line.

Write in accordance with preceding rule, omitting the vowels and *all* consonants *not* sounded:

Pea	me	cue	pity	poor	pig	pitch
eel	itch	new	meal	coop	doom	loop
few	ill	pick	boom	cure	chip	lure

§ 18. The *outline* or skeleton of a word is *always* written without lifting the pencil from the paper. But when initial diphthong *I* is joined it must be written first; thus,   *mentally,*   *Ida.*

§ 19. A straight consonant is repeated by doubling its length; thus, _____ *kay-kay,* _____ *gay-gay.*

§ 20. Curved stems are repeated by making the signs twice; thus,   *ef-ef,*   *dhe-dhe.*

§ 21. There should always be an angle between *ef* and *en, ve* and *en, ve* and *ing, le* and *em, emp-b* and *ess.*

§ 22. There should be no angle between *pe-en, ith-en, ef-kay, de-ef, le-ess, le-er, le-ish, le-she, em-ess.*

§ 23. Light and heavy stems that do not form an angle at their junction when joined should be so blended that the precise point of juncture is not discernible; thus,   *b-p,*   *b-n,*   *p-ng.*

§ 24. As will be seen by reference to the tables, the *first-place* vowel and diphthong sounds are *a* as in *calm, a* as in *ball, a* as in *bat, o* as in *on, i* as in *ice, oy* as in *boy,* and *ow* as in *cow.* The *second-place* sounds are *a* as in *fade, o* as in *lode, e* as in *bet,* and *u* as in *up.*

The *third-place* sounds are *ea* as in *peal,* *i* as in *pit,* *oo* in *foot,* *oo* in *food,* and *ew* in *view.* When these different sounds are so clearly impressed in the mind that when a word is spoken the position or place of its accented vowel is readily determined, then the student has but little further use for the vowels; they need not be inserted the first perpendicular or inclined stem of the word being written in the position of its accented vowel, makes it intelligible. Let us take a few words for illustration; thus, in the word *balm* the consonant sounds are B and M, and the vowel long *a* as in *calm,* which occupies a first place, therefore we should write it, ＼— *balm;* *cap* has a first-place vowel and the consonants should be written above the line, thus, ＼*cap, fowl,* consonants F and L, diphthong *ow* r first-place sound, and therefore should be written, ＞ *fowl;* *shade,* consonants SH and D, vowel long *a,* second-place, so we write it, ⌐ *shade; rub,* having a second-place sound, we write, ∧ *rub; poke,* second-place vowel, ＼— *poke; poem,* accented vowel, second-place, write it, ＼— *poem;* words like *iota* and *idea* should be vocalized; thus, ⌡ *iota,* ⌡ʻ *idea.* In several of the preceding illustrations, and in some which will be hereafter presented, it will be noticed that the words are vocalized. This is done merely to show those who may wish to write according to the old method of first teaching the "Corresponding Style," or who may experience difficulty in associating the sounds and position, the method in vogue for the insertion of the vowels. This, however, cannot be recommended, as it has been found by actual practice that students make more rapid and easy progress by simply memorizing the different vowel sounds and their corresponding positions in reference to the line of writing, omitting the vowels and writing the consonants of the word in the manner already explained.

RULES FOR WRITING SH, L, AND R.

§ 25. When SH is the first consonant stem in a word that begins with a vowel, when it is the only consonant in a word, or when it is the final element of a word write the down stroke; ⁄ *show,* ⟨ *Ashby,* ⟩ *push.*

§ 26. When SH is the last consonant in a word that ends with a vowel sound write it upward; but in the middle and at the beginning of words the upward or downward stroke may be employed; thus, ⟍⁀ *bushy*, ⟋ *sure*, ⟨ *shabby*.

§ 27. When L is the first consonant sound in a word that begins with a vowel and is next followed by a horizontal stem, or when it is the final element of a word the down stroke should be used; thus, ⟋ *alum*, ⟩ *boil*.

§ 28. When L is the only consonant stem in a word, when it begins a word, when it is the last consonant in a word that ends with a vowel sound, or when it is the first consonant in the word and is followed by a down stroke stem the L should be written upward; thus, / *ail*, ⟍⟋ *fellow*, /⟍ *lope*.

§ 29. In the middle of words L may be written either upward or downward, but the upstroke generally gives the best outline.

§ 30. After N it is generally best to write the L downward and after M upward whether followed by a vowel or not, as better outlines are given; thus, ⟋ *inlay*.

§ 31. When R begins a word, when it is the last consonant in a word that ends with a vowel sound, and always before *ith*, *dhe*, *chay* and *jay* the stem Ree should be used; thus, ⟋ *to-morrow*, ⟋-*wreath*, ⟋ *wreathe*, ⟋ *rich*, ⟋ *rage*, ⟍⟋ *ferry*.

§ 32. When R is the first or only consonant in a word that begins with a vowel, when it is the final element of the word, and always before M use the downstroke R; thus, ⟍ *air*, ⟍ *cur*, ⟍ *roam*.

§ 33. In the middle of words either the upward or downward R may be used, but the upstroke is generally the best. When R follows R or stroke H the upward R should be used; thus, ⟋ *roar*.

SIGNS FOR H.

§ 34. The stroke H is used in the following cases:

I. When H is the only consonant or the only one that can be conveniently represented by a stroke.

II. For initial H preceding a consonant followed by a vowel.

§ 35. In reporting the H is omitted from such words as hope, happy, had, have, half; thus, ⌐ *heap*, ＼ *hope*.

§ 36. Before M, L, R, stroke S or a hook, H is expressed by a small heavy perpendicular tick; thus, ⌐ *home*, ⌐ *whole*.

SIGNS FOR W AND Y.

§ 37. The stroke stems for W and Y are used when W or Y is the only consonant in the word, or when it is the first consonant in a word that begins with a vowel; thus, ＼ *way*, ＼ *awake*.

§ 38. A small semi-circle is employed as an additional sign for these letters. For W it opens to the right or left, and for Y either upward or downward; they are generally employed when W or Y is the initial sound in the word, or when immediately followed by D; ＼ *web*, ⌐ *wash*, | *wood*.

§ 39. W may be prefixed to Lee and Ree by a large initial hook; and to M and N by a small initial hook; thus, ⌐ *whale*, ⌐ *weary*, ⌐ *won*. The phrases *we will, we are, we may* and *we know* may be expressed by wL, wR, wM, and wN, respectively. These words occur very frequently in connection with other words in phrases, and this method of denoting them adds greatly to the speed and beauty of the writing. *We-will-be*, written wL²-B; *we²-may-go*, wM²-G; *we-know-you-are*, wR-diphthong u-Ree; *we-are-now*, wR-N.

READING EXERCISE No. 1.

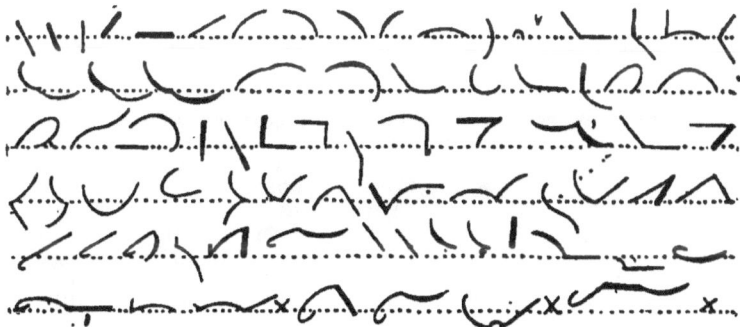

KEY.

Line 1.—Pea, be, tea, jay, gay, ray, ell, err, way, yea, Em, see, you, I, p-k, d-p, t-m, ch-p.

Line 2.—F-n, v-n, v-ing, l-m, mp-z, p-n, f-g, d-f, l-s, l-r.

Line 3.—L-sh, l-sh, m-s, d-t, p-b, decay, Katy, pity, empty, gale, envy, pekay, cage.

Line 4.—Shape, fish, fishy, alike, fell, fellow, leap, bulk, mail, fear, erry, rage, urge, rope.

Line 5.—Hero, Hay, hazy, hear, held, hang, happy, hope, have, half, had, awake, week, one.

Line 6.—We may go home to-morrow. We will be willing if you are. We are going.

WRITING EXERCISE No. 1.

WRITE IN FIRST POSITION IN ACCORDANCE WITH § 15.

Odd	pa	paw	bow	ought	awl	thou
at	am	add	taw	daw	my	maw
mow	chaw	jaw	caw	thaw	saw	shaw
law	alm	gnaw	ha	haw	odd	off
ash	pie	boy	bough	buy	tie	die
now	cow	why	shy	guy	annoy	oil

WRITE IN SECOND POSITION IN ACCORDANCE WITH § 16.

Pay	bay	beau	Abe	dough	toe	mow
foe	Joe	low	fay	they	though	show
ode	aid	owed	gay	lay	up	Ed
egg	etch	Em	know	air	err	oar

WRITE IN THIRD POSITION IN ACCORDANCE WITH § 17.

Pea	be	tea	eat	key	fee	eve
see	ooze	she	me	lee	itch	eel
knee	woo	ye	he	it	chew	few
view	new	use	mew	she		

WRITE IN PROPER POSITION IN ACCORDANCE WITH § 15-17.

Paw	day	lieu	ail	gay	awed	dough
eke	foe	thee	thaw	ape		ate
nay	eaze	if	own	in	on	say
so	ace	way	lie	Jew	nigh	ache
out	by	day	each	joy	if	age
few	thy	saw	so	say	us	ease
may	no	know	allow	see	easy	ill

§ 40. SIMPLE CONSONANT WORD SIGNS.

In the following table of word signs the word in the upper part of the brace is written in the first position, the one in the middle in the second position, and the lower one in the third position. The words in italic are not grammalogues or word signs, but simply words written in the "Reporting Style."

╲	{ *happy* plaintiff *pea*	╱	{ shall, shalt *show* *shoe*
│	{ *at* what *it*	╱	{ usual-ly
╻	{ *had* defendant, do did	⌒	{ time member *me*
╱	{ charge change, which *each*	⌣	{ *on* *no* any
╱	{ large advantage *Jew*	⌣	{ long young thing
▬	{ can come could	⌢	{ important-ance may be improve-d-ment
▬	{ go gave give-n	╱	{ our, are *ray* *rue*
╲	{ form *foe* *if*	╲	{ *why* *way* woo
)	{ was whose	╱	{ beyond *yea*
(	{ thank youth think		

§ 41. VOWEL WORD SIGNS.

• a ⚫ an ′and . the ` all ′oh, owe, ⁄ who ╲ but
╲ to ⁄ should ⌢ how ⌒ you ⸦ with ⁊ we ` of
⸦ would.

Should and *and* are always written upward.

TICKS AND JOINING OF WORDS.

§ 42. *The,* the most frequent occurring word in the English language, may be expressed by a short tick preferably in the direction of CH, but sometimes in the direction of Ree, joined to the preceding word. The tick *the* never begins a word; thus, ⌣ *on the,* ＞ *to the,* ႗ *as the.*

§ 43. *A* or *an* is joined to the preceding word by a small perpendicular or horizontal tick; *of* and *a,* and *to* and *a,* should not be joined but must be written separately; thus, ⌐ *can a,* ⌐ *on a,*

§ 44. *He* may be written initially or finally by a heavy tick; thus, ＼ *if he,* ⌐ *can he,* ＼ *he was.*

§ 45. *I* is generally represented by the diphthong I, but may be abbreviated by writing only the first stroke, when it will join easily to the consonant; thus, ↑ *I had,* ⌣ *I may.*

§ 46. The principle of joining ticks may also be applied to all word signs that join well. The first word must always be written in position, and *no* and *go* should be vocalized to distinguish them from *any* and *come;* thus, ＼ *can be,* ⌒ *you may go.*

§ 47. The connective phrase *of the* is intimated by writing the words between which it occurs near to each other; thus, ⌒ *importance of the improvement.*

WRITING EXERCISE No. 2.

If the student desires to "vocalize"—*i. e.* place the vowels to the consonant stems—he may do so in accordance with §§ 7-10, and the following rules : 1. *First-place* vowels are written at the beginning of consonant strokes ; *second-place* in the middle, and *third place* at the end, so in up-strokes the first-place would be at the *beginning* (apparently at the bottom) of the stroke and third-place at the *end* (or apparently at the top) of the stroke. 2. *All first-place* and *long second-place* vowels are written to the stem which precedes them ; *short second place* and *all third-place* vowels are written to the stem which follows them.

We would suggest to the instructor or student that when the words in the various exercises are written for the first time the outlines should not be vocalized, but put in proper position

.according to ₴ 14. In reviewing, the outlines may be vocalized, if desired, but it is not necessary.

It is entirely unnecessary to vocalize the outlines, as in actual reporting the vowels are never inserted except occasionally in proper names and words of infrequent use.

WRITE IN FIRST POSITION IN ACCORDANCE WITH ₴ 15.

Pack	palm	pang	pattie	pop	back	tack
patch	path	bag	body	chop	type	job
dime	dodge	dam	damp	dock	daub	sham
jam	cap	camp	cabbage	Chicago	catch	couch
occupy						

WRITE IN SECOND POSITION IN ACCORDANCE WITH ₴ 16.

Pope	penny	poach	poke	poem	money	puffy
bake	bevy	death	take	make	marry	funny
foam	came	jump	bump	fame.	tame	toney
game	dome					

WRITE IN THIRD POSITION IN ACCORDANCE WITH ₴ 17.

peep	duty	pity	doom	cheap	dizzy	keep
coop	nip	pig	jib	tip	nick	kick
ink	kink	mink	chick	cube	boom	
neap	zinc					

WRITE IN PROPER POSITION, OBSERVING THE RULES, ₴₴ 25-33.

she	shop	push	bushy	shadow	shame	issue
bishop	mash	dash	alike	along	illume	coil
alcohol	fall	ball	fuel	nail	bill	ail
lay	lap	like	lung	fellow	folly	pillow
mellow	bulk	utility	outlive	inlay	kneel	mile
annually	annual	newly	mail	meal	mule	ray
rope	rotary	ridge	reach.	retailer	air	ore
arm	arrive	fear	ferry	Arab	rear	pork
career	parody					

WRITE IN ACCORDANCE WITH ₴ 34.

Hang	hang	hap	harp	Harry	harsh	hash
Harvey	Harriet	hatch	hate	haughty	havoc	hay
knife	he	heavy	heretic	hero	herring	hewed
hewer	hop	honey	hindoo	horrify	horrid	hoop
hub	hung					

WRITE IN ACCORDANCE WITH ₴ 35.

Had	half	have	hope	happy	harm	hath

WRITE IN ACCORDANCE WITH ₴ 36.

Hail	hair	hall	whole	ham	him	hear
her	hawk	hog	hack	home	here	heel
hem	hemp	hominy	homily	howl	hulk	hull
humbug	hump	humming				

WRITE IN ACCORDANCE WITH §§ 37-39.

Way	weigh	why	woo	yale	ye	awake
away	awoke	by-way	wake	week	wish	watch
wage	wager	wait	wug	waive	walk	wife
widow	width	wide	yoke	yacht	wail	wan
one	win	window	warm	winch	war	wall
well	will	wool	willing	whale	work	were
where	warp	wary	whereon	wire		

SENTENCES.

[The words in *italics* in the sentences of all the writing exercises should be joined; but if there is an x between two words they must not be connected. The connective phrase, *of the,* occurring in the middle of a sentence, is never written, but is expressed by writing the words between which it occurs near to each other. Indicate *the, a,* and *an,* wherever possible, by the tick sign.]

What *can you* give me if I will come?
I shall give you an important charge.
I am weary of doing nothing and *shall go* home to-morrow.
You may be willing to *become a* member.
How long *shall you* be *among them?*
*I will be among them a*x*long time.*
Charge me with *what you* have *given them.*
You should do nothing *at any time you* fear *would be wrong.*
We will ship you to-day in shape, the sheep we *wish you* x *to take.*

S AND Z CIRCLE.

§ 48. The S and Z sounds are of such frequent occurrence that it has been found necessary to give them additional and briefer signs (small circles), and ones which are more convenient for joining. The "ess-circle," so called to distinguish it from the stroke S, ·), is employed much more frequently than the latter. Except as word sign, it is used only in connection with stroke consonants. Aside from its brevity it furnishes a graceful and fluent method of joining both straight and curved stems, preserving lineality of writing and apparently infusing life and expression into the notes.

§ 49. The circle is joined:

I. To single straight stems by a motion from the right over to the left.

II. To simple curved stems by writing it inside the curve.

§ 50. TABLE OF THE CIRCLE S.

⸜ aPs	⸜ sBs	ʅ sTs	ʅ sDs	⸝ sCHs	⸝ sJs
⸍ sKs	⸍ sGs	⸜ sFs	⸜ sVs	ʆ sTHs	ʆ sDH
ꝫ sSs	ꝫ sZs	ꝭ sSHs	ꝭ sZHs	⸝ sLs	ꝭ sRs
⸍ sMs	⸍ sNs	⸍ sNGs	ꝭ sWs	⸝ sYs	⸍ sMPs
ℓ Hs	⸝ sRs	⸝ swLs	⸝ swRs	⸍ swMs	⸍ swNs

By referring to the table it will be seen that there are two ways of indicating *sr*, one by the circle on the downstroke R and the other by the circle on Ree. The first should be employed when *r* is preceded by a vowel sound, as in *soar*, and the latter when the *r* is followed by a vowel sound, as in *sorrow*.

§ 51. When the ess-circle occurs between two strokes, if there be no angle at their junction, it is written to the first stem as if it stood alone; but if there be an angle, it is written on the outer side of the angle; thus, —•— *ksk*; ⸜— *fsm*.

§ 52. The circle may be used at the beginning, in the middle and at the end of words; thus, ⸜ *sap*, ⸍ *unsafe*, ⸝ *peas*.

§ 53. A circle is read first, therefore if a vowel is the first sound of a word use the stroke S, or if a words ends with a vowel sound use the stroke.

§ 54. In upstrokes initial ess is at the bottom and the final circle at the top; thus, ⸝ *sail*, ⸝ *lace*.

§ 55. L with an initial circle when standing alone is *always* written upward, and *SH* downward. When *s* occurs between L and N, or L and V, the L is *always* written downward.

§ 56. When a word contains no other consonant the stroke S or Z is used; thus,) *ace*, ⸍ *ease*.

§ 57. When S or Z is the last consonant sound in a word that ends with a vowel the stem sign should be used; thus, ⸝) *racy*, ⸝) *rosy*.

§ 58. When S or Z is immediately followed or immediately preceded by two concurrent vowels the stem sign should be used; thus, ⸜ *essence*, ⸝ *science*.

§ 59. When two ess sounds are the only consonants in a word
one should be written with the circle and the other with a stem
sign. An initial circle should be used in words that end with a
vowel sound, and a final circle in those words that end with the
sound of ess ; thus, -ɔ̣- *cease,* ℈ *sissy.*

§ 60. When S is the first consonant in a word that begins with
a vowel the stem sign should be used ; thus, ℔ *assume.*

§ 61. When Z is the first consonant sound in a word, whether
there be an initial vowel or not, the stem sign should be used ;
thus, ℣ *zero.*

§ 62. When the sounds of *s* and *z* occur in connection with some
other consonant, in such syllables as *ses, sis, cis, sus, sys, cise, zes,*
they may be represented by a large circle twice the size for *s.*

, § 63. The large circle is joined to consonant stems the same as
the small one, and may be used at the beginning, in the middle
and at the end of words ; thus, ℔ *system,* ⍾ *necessity,* ℅ *bases.*

. § 64. Although seldom necessary, the vowel or diphthong occurring between the two consonants represented by the large circle
may be expressed by writing it inside the hook ; thus, ⟋ᵖ *exhaust.*

ST AND STR LOOPS.

· § 65. When T immediately follows S, or D follows Z, the sounds
are represented by a small loop about one-third the length of the
stem. When the sounds of *z* and *d* are preceded by only one consonant then the circle *s* and stroke *d* must be used ; if, however,
these sounds are preceded by two or more consonants then the
st-loop may be used.

§ 66. The sound of *str* with any intervening vowel is represented by a large loop extending about two-thirds the length of the
stem.

· § 67. The st-loop may be used at the beginning, in the middle
and at the end, and the str-loop in the middle and at the end of
words ; thus, ＼ *step,* ├─ *destiny,* ＼ *best,* ├─ *duster,* ⌒ *master,* ⍾ *yesterday.*

· § 68. S may be added to the large circle and to the *st* and *str*
loops by turning a small circle on the opposite side of the stem ;
thus, ℔ *possesses,* ℣ *boasts,* ℅ *boasters.*

· § 69. *As, has, is* or *his* may be added initially and finally to
other words, and *us* finally, by the ess-circle, or by making a

circle beginning or ending a word into a large circle; thus, ᴗᴗ *as long as,* ʃ *has had,* ᴗᴗ *is in,* ᴗᴗ *as soon as.*

§ 70. *As is, as his, as has, has his, his is, is as* may be joined initially and finally to other words by the large circle; thus, ᴗᴗ *as has no.*

§ 71. *Is it* is prefixed to words or word signs by writing a small detached loop and joining it to the following consonant; thus, ⌒ *is it now.*

§ 72. *There, their* or *they are* is added to the ess-circle word signs by making the circle into a large loop and joining it to the following stem; thus, ⌒ *as there can be,* ⌒ *as there is now.*

§ 73. The circle *ess* may be added to any consonant sign to represent the plural or the possessive case of nouns, or the third person singular of verbs; thus, ᴗ *its,* ᴗ *comes,* ᴗ *does.*

§ 74. Between S and another consonant T may be omitted; thus, ᴗ *must be,* ᴗ *postage,* ᴗ *postmaster.*

§ 75. CIRCLE WORD SIGNS.

as, has / self / is, his	several / *sieve*
as i, has is, as has, has as / selves / is as, his is, is his	similarity / *same* / similar
sap / special-ly / *soup*	*nice* / *owns* / insurance
because / *case* / *keys*	honest / next
sag / signify	impossible / improvements
fast / first / *feast*	*song* / singular

READING EXERCISE No. 2.

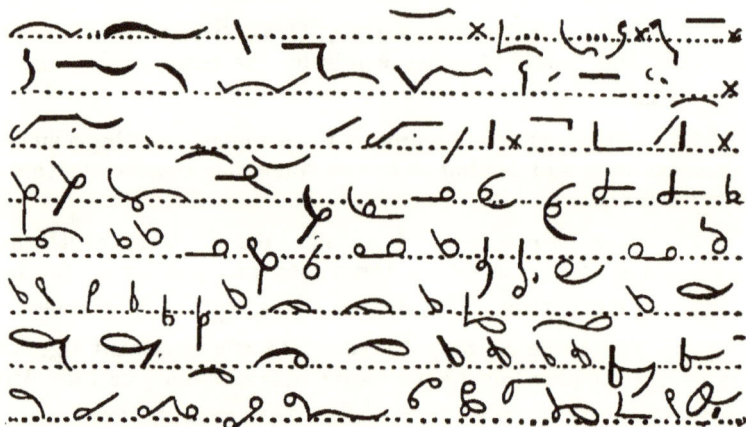

KEY.

Line 1.—May the money be given them now? It may be if you wish. If he can.

Line 2.—He was going away to-morrow, but will now wait and go with me.

Line 3.—We are going to improve in our work each day. Can he take charge of the defendant?

Line 4.—Upset, passage, f-s-m, gasp, visage, physic, case, lesson, illusive, task, desk, oats.

Line 5.—Chasm, pass, passes, cases, subsist, chooses, success, possess, disease, decease, season, Sussex, horse.

Line 6.—Past, stop, state, toast, teas, teased, pastor, must, muster, post, teamster, minister, poster, strong.

Line 7.—Strength, strange, impost, impose, imposter, boaster, boasters, post, posters, distinguish, destiny.

Line 8.—Store, story, surface, serious, ceremony, as well as, as fast as, as it can, postmaster, ask, special, as there is no.

WRITING EXERCISE No. 3.

WRITE IN ACCORDANCE WITH §§ 49-50.

Stay	stow	sit	city	said	suit
sack	sank	safe	safely	fees	seen
sun	some	pass	face	soap	peace

office	sang	soar	sorry	series	sale
sales	saves	seems	source	oppose	service
ceremony	base	pays	piece	seed	abuse
buys	sat	ties	toss	ages	side
sad	such	choose	joys	those	cause
accuse	case	saith	south	allows	this
thus	laws	loss	less	amuse	lose
soul	seal	arise	amaze	news	knows
sing	song	owns			

WRITE IN ACCORDANCE WITH ¿ 51.

Cask	mask	task	desk	physic	phasma
noisily	upset	opposite	officer	sincere	sincerely
music	dusty	pasty	misty	chisel	hasty
haystack	lesser	misery	miser	mislay	resign

WRITE IN ACCORDANCE WITH ¿¿ 55-61.

Sail	shows	illusive	allusive	elusive	lesson
license	listen	loosen	looseness	ask	asp
assay	aspire	escape	assail	fussy	mossy
busy	lazy	easy	dizzy	noisy	assassin
science	assignees	zion	zany	zero	easily
user	sauce	seize	says	size	seize

WRITE IN ACCORDANCE WITH ¿ 63.

Passes	bosses	possess	success	causes	masses
faces	vases	chooses	basis	laces	insist
necessary	possessed	Sussex	submissive		

WRITE IN ACCORDANCE WITH ¿¿ 65-68.

Stop	stake	stoop	stool	steam	stamp
stair	stock	store	story	stencil	past
based	taste	cost	most	lost	fast
missed	chaste	must	waste	haste	based
rest	arrest	post	passed	tossed	test
state	stout	steed	stood	stead	just
coast	cast	style	steal	still	stole
stale	justify	mystify	poster	master	castor
faster `	teamster	waster	baluster	chests	roasters
attests	possesses	successes	teamsters	costs	disturb

SENTENCES.

[When *we*, with another word is enclosed in [ ], it denotes that the *we* is to be expressed by the *w*-hook.]

It is impossible to *see the* defendant *as his case* comes up to-day.

[*We will*] *ship you* to-day the things *sold you* yesterday, and mail you invoice and bill, which pay *as soon as* you can.

It is best to think well ere we speak.

It cost much money but it caused success to visit our store, and stay with us.

It is singular but *he was* the first to come.

As a usual thing *we have* to pay cash, but *when they* sold us the last load *they said you may* take *as long as* you wish to *pay the* bill; we would thank all firms for similar services.

As there is no hope of your selling *anything, I think* x *it is* folly *to stay among them.*

Have you any bill which James & Smith refused to pay? If so, [*we will*] *take* it and sue them *if you* desire.

When *you are in the* city come and see us, and [*we will*] *show you a* nice stock.

As *we are* selling our stock so cheap—almost giving it away—we think *it would be* to your advantage to purchase now.

No one is always right, sometimes we all err.

Always do *what you* x *think is* right, if by so doing *you will injure* x *no one.*

L AND R HOOKS.

§ 76. The simple articulations, *p, b, t, d,* etc., are so closely united with *l* and *r* that they form a kind of consonant diphthong, pronounced by a single effort of the organs of speech. Take for instance the words *play, plow, flow,* and notice how the *l* imperceptibly glides into the *p* and seemingly with but one effort of the vocal organs; and in the words *pray, prow, fray, gray, bray,* the same may be said of the *pr, fr, gr, br.* In writing, the natural way of expressing these combinations would undoubtedly be by some marked and uniform modification of the simple letters, and so in Short-hand they are expressed by simple, yet distinct and uniform modifications of the consonants: a small initial hook on the circle side of straight stems for *l* and on the opposite side for *r.* The *l* and *r*-hook combinations are used when the *l* and *r* blend with the preceding consonant, and when no, or but a slightly perceptible vowel sound occurs between them. They must not be understood to represent the sounds *per, ber, ker, ger, pel, bel, kel,* etc., but rather the sounds *pri* (short i), *bri, kri, pli, bli, kli,* etc., the former being written with stroke signs. In words like *play, free, apple, upper,* the hook combinations may be used, but in such words as *pail, fear, pile, poor,* the stroke signs should be employed.

§ 77. A small hook on the circle side and at the beginning of any stem except S, Z, R, L, M, N, NG, MP-B, W and H. and a large initial hook on N, M, NG and MP-B indicates that L follows.

§ 78. SH1 and ZH1 have their hooks at the bottom, are always written upward and never stand alone.

§ 79. A small hook at the beginning and on the side opposite the el-hook on straight stems, except Ree and H, adds R. The addition of an R on curved stems (except S, Z, L, R, M, N, NG, W and Y) is indicated by turning over sideways the corresponding L-hook signs, except SH1 and ZH1, which are turned over endways.

§ 80. SHr and ZHr have their hooks at the top and are always written downward.

§ 81. R may be added to M and N by a small initial hook, provided the M and N are first thickened, as NG and MP never take an initial R-hook. R may be added to L by a small initial hook.

§ 82. TABLE OF THE L HOOK SIGNS.

ᒉ Pl	ᒉ Bl	ᒉ Tl	ᒉ Dl	ᒉ CHl	ᒉ Jl
ᒉ Kl	ᒉ Gl	ᒉ Fl	ᒉ Vl	ᒉ THl	ᒉ DHl
ᒉ SHl	ᒉ ZHl	ᒉ Ml	ᒉ Nl	ᒉ NGl	ᒉ Yl
ᒉ MPl	ᒉ Rl				

§ 83. TABLE OF THE R HOOK SIGNS.

ᒉ Pr	ᒉ Br	ᒉ Tr	ᒉ Dr	ᒉ CHr	ᒉ Jr
ᒉ Kr	ᒉ Gr	ᒉ Fr	ᒉ Vr	ᒉ THr	ᒉ DHr
ᒉ SHr	ᒉ ZHr	ᒉ Mr	ᒉ Nr	ᒉ Lr	

§ 84. The L and R hooks though made at the beginning are read after, not before the stem; thus, ᒉ *play*, ᒉ *pray*.

§ 85. The L and R hook combinations are used for such close blendings of L or R following consonants, as occur at the beginning of the words clay, fry, prow; but even in such words as apple, evil, copper, where the sounds are separated by a slight vowel the hooks are used, but in words like *pail*, *fear*, etc,, where a distinct vowel sound occurs, the stem signs must be used.

§ 86. In some cases when an L or R hook sign is joined to a preceding letter the hook cannot be perfectly formed, in such cases a slight offset of the pen serves instead of the hook; thus,

ᒉ *reply*, ᒉ *tiger*, ᒉ *gospel*, ᒉ *registry*.

WRITING EXERCISE No. 4.

[An "1" before *all* or *will* denotes that the *all* or *will* is to be expressed by an *l*-hook on the preceding stem; and an "r" between two words denotes that the word immediately following the "r" is expressed by the *r*-hook on the preceding stem.]

WRITE IN ACCORDANCE WITH §§ 77–85.

Play	try	agree	pry	plumes	placed
flow	true	dray	only	fro	blooms
pleased	plow	drew	grasp	draw	free.
appraised	flaw	apply	drayage	crow	frame
plush	pleasing	able	apples	trial	cry
brew	applause	glass	glue	blue	throw
frail	plaster	cluster	glaze		

WRITE IN ACCORDANCE WITH § 85.

Outer	fear	coil	powder	impress	authorized
acre	utter	gear	pile	pitcher	buckle
honor	usher	author	lower	bills	barrels
trouble	ample	azure	owner	jewels	reaper
purely	tackle	angles	pickles	offer	bushel
jobber	proper	staple	bevel	inner	fall
measure	rubber	copper			

WRITE IN ACCORDANCE WITH § 86.

Liable	durable	degree	broker	nickel	brokerage
honorable	allowable	cable	taker	maker	maple
cheaper	deliver	legal	enable	couple	shipper
applicable					

SENTENCES.

I shall draw on you *at three days' sight,* x *please have the* money ready.

Owe *no one,* and ask *no one to* x *trust* you.

Friday is looked upon *as an* unlucky day.

It l *will be impossible* x *to ship you the* bushel measures by next Saturday, *but* l *will try* and ship them Monday.

I shall be pleased x to *mail* x *you our price list,* and solicit your custom.

[*We will*] *deliver* your copper next month, if possible.

Speak the truth so people *will have* faith in your word.

A number *of* r *our* customers will arrive to-morrow.

The offers were *mostly from local buyers.*

You should try and employ time *to the best* advantage.

I have nothing to say, please *ask them.*

The prices *you make* me are too high.

¿ 87. To avoid long and inconvenient outlines an L or R hook may be used, even if a distinct vowel sound occurs between the stem and the L or R.

PROPER EMPLOYMENT OF THE L AND R HOOKS.

¿ 88. When there is a distinct vowel sound between the consonant and the L or R the stroke signs should be used instead of the L or R hooks. The hook combinations should be retained for the natural blendings of the L and R with other stems. By so doing the notes will be more easily read and the speed increased. If, however, the outline would be too long, awkward, or extend too far below the line, the hook should be used. The hook for R should be used in the middle of words when that consonant is followed by M, as the down stroke would carry the outline too far below the line; thus, Tr²-M-Ns, *terminus*, P²-R-sN, *person*, Pr³-ssT, *persist*. *Full* is best written Fl³. The hooks should be used on stems that have final hooks followed by another stem, when if the stem L or R was used the final hook could not be employed, or if it was would make the outline too long or inconvenient. The list of words which should have an L or R hook instead of the stem sign, given in the latter part of the book, will be of great help to the student, as it contains all the words in common use which take this special vocalization.

¿ 89. S is prefixed to all the L hook stems, to R on curves, and to the W hook by writing the circle inside the hook.

¿ 90. S is prefixed to straight R hook stems by making the hook into a small circle, *ses* by making the hook into a large circle, and *st* by making the hook into a small loop.

¿ 91. SPl SERIES OF CONSONANTS.

sPl sBl sTl sDl sCHl sJl
sKl sGl sF sVl sTHl sDHl
ssHl sZHl sMl sNl sNGl sYl
sMPl sRl

¿ 92. sPr AND sW SERIES OF CONSONANTS.

sPr sBr sTr sDr sCHr sJr
sKr sGr sFr sVr sTHr sDHr
sSHr sZHr sMr sNr sLr

§ 93. A word written with an L or R hook stem is read as follows: First, the initial circle or loop; second, vowels before the stem; third, the stem with its hook and intervening vowel, if there be one; and fourth, any vowel after the stem.

§ 94. In the middle of words, where possible, the circle and hook of the double letter must be distinctly expressed; thus, ⟍ *excursive*, ⌊ *disclose.*

§ 95. After T, D, B and P, the circle may be turned to the right to form the treble consonants sKr, sGr; thus, ⌊ *disgrace*, ⌊ *disagree.*

§ 96. Students of Phonography generally experience trouble in writing words where the first consonants are *s, t* and *r;* their first impulse being to express this combination according to the *spr*-series of consonants—by turning a small circle on the *r*-hook side of the consonant T—whether a vowel sound comes between the *st* and *r* or not. In words like *string, strung, strong, strength, strange* and *strangle,* the *str*-loop may be employed to express this combination. When a distinct vowel sound is heard between the *st* and *r,* in such words as *store, storm, stork,* then the *st*-loop and downstroke R should be used. In words like *straight, strap, stricken,* etc., where the *st* and *r* naturally blend, and even if the *s* was omitted a complete word would be left, a circle should be turned on the *r*-hook side of T to form the *str.*

§ 97. The syllable *in, en* or *un* may be affixed to the sPr series by turning a small backward hook on the L hook side of the stem, and at the beginning of any other stroke, to avoid turning a circle on the convex side of N by a small back hook on the outside of the curve; thus, ⟍ *inscribe,* ⌊ *unstrung,* ⟋ *enslave.*

§ 98. *All* or *will* may be added by the L hook; thus ⌠ *at all,* ⌠ *they will.*

§ 99. *Are* or *our* may be added by the R hook; thus, ⟍ *they are soon.*

§ 100. L AND R HOOK SERIES WORD SIGNS.

⎮ *during*[3], ⟋ *largely*[1], ⎮ *truth*[2], ⟍ *principal-le*[3], ⟍ *number*[2], ⟋ *larger*[1].

§ 101. A large number of words contain the combinations *qu* and *gu,* which in Phongraphy are equivalent to *kw* and *gw;* and there are also a large number of words in which *t* and *d* are followed by *w*, as in *acquire, quest, dwell, twist.* This sound of *w, is* expressed by a large initial hook on the *l*-hook side of these consonants, but unlike the *w*-hook on L, R, M and N, is read after not before the stem; thus, ∫⋯ *twist,* ⌐⟍ *queer,* ⟋⋅⟍ *require.*

READING EXERCISE No. 3.

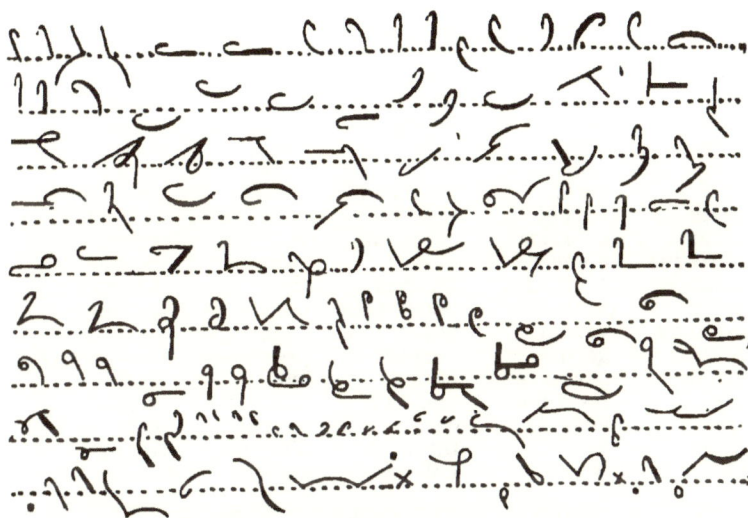

KEY.

Line 1.—Play, pray, pale, pare, clay, glow, flow, fray, tray, dray, evil, oval, other, their, yell, ethel, more.

Line 2.—Outer, aider, over, near, inner, honor, only, eager, usher, shrew, owner, reply, tiger, tipple.

Line 3.—Gospel, registry, register, couple, cooper, real, roller, bushel, treasure, preacher.

Line 4.—Camel, trapper, angle, ample, rumor, flay, fail, small, tell, till, dear, care, full.

Line 5.—Coarse, call, courage, term, persist, their, person, personal, fulfill, Turk, dark

Line 6.—Charm, term, thirsty, thirst, perform, purple, supply, splice, sable, civil, single, simple, sample, school.

Line 7.—Suffer, spry, spray, seeker, cedar, sister, physical, feasible, disagreeable, disgrace, sting, strap, storm.

Line 8.—Insoluble, unscrew, it will be, they are able, of our, of all, all our, all will, to all, to our, who are, who will, should all, should our, and our-are, and all-will, queer, require, twist, inquiry.

Line 9.—The principal number of the firm will arrive to-morrow. Honesty is the best policy. The number is wrong.

WRITING EXERCISE No. 5.

WRITE IN ACCORDANCE WITH §§ 87–88.

Tell	till	dear	cheer	call
care	for	cur	sure	more
mere	nor	near	curse	course
their	there	rail	real	rule
chair	roll	verse	thirst	thirsty
nurse	term	terminus	turkey	portray
perish	parcel	calcine	culminate	collect
colony	colonize	corporal	courage	cornice
courteous	correct	cursed	carnage	corner
garner	garnish	furnace	thirty	Charles
surely	moral	occurrence	charm	purple
Germany	verbal	polity	attorneys	perfumer
perhaps	germ	perjure	preverse	telegraphy
perspire	perceive	parley	barely	dark
turmoil	terminate	eternity	adverse	kernal
dirk	jerk	curdle	coarse	girl
ignore	girdle	furlough	Thursday	reality
shark	incur	college	realize	

WRITE IN ACCORDANCE WITH §§ 89–93.

Supply	splice	settle	saddle	sickle
satchel	civil	school	sample	single
spry	spray	sober	straw	cedar
screw	sooner	stager	suffer	sperm
suppress	supper	spruce	spring	sable
stopper	stagger	scrap	scruples	scratch

WRITE IN ACCORDANCE WITH § 94.

Possible	feasible	visible	display	displace
disable	plausible	traceable	disclose	disclaim
prosper	destroy	extra	extreme	tapestry
abstruse	displeased	distrust	dishonor	example
mystery	registry	rasper	prisoner	

WRITE IN ACCORDANCE WITH § 95.

Prescribe	proscribe	obscure	discry	disagreeable
describe	describer	subscribe	subscriber	disgraced
disgorge				

WRITE IN ACCORDANCE WITH § 96.

String	strung	strange	strong	strength
strangle	star	store	story	steer
storage	storm	stir	sterling	strap
straw	straddle	strap	stretch	stretcher
strike	struck	stripe	struggle	stroke

WRITE IN ACCORDANCE WITH § 97.

Unscrew	unseemly	unsociable	inscribe	insolvable
inseparable	unsalable	unscrupulous		

WRITE IN ACCORDANCE WITH § 101.

Twist	quest	twill	dwell	quell
queer	require	acquire	quire	square

SENTENCES.

It gives me pleasure *to mail* x *you our terms* on *railroad supplies.*
They r *are* very cheap *at the* price given.
There is no place like home.
He who can bridle his tongue wins the approval *of* l *all.*
I shall endeavor x *to come* x *since this is* the case, but *he must* also
appear.
It is the way *in which* things *are said many times* x *which makes them*
so disagreeable.
You must x *obey the* laws of health *if you* x *would be well.*

FINAL HOOKS.

F, V AND N HOOKS.

§ 102. *F* or *v* may be added to any straight stem, whether it be
simple or have an initial circle loop or hook, by a *small* final hook
on the right-hand or *ess*-circle side, and *n* by a *small* final hook
on the opposite side.

§ 103. N may be added to any curved stem by a *small* final hook
on the inner side of the curve. The *v*-hook is never used on a
curved stem except to add *of, have* or *ever,* as it would be difficult
to distinguish it from *n.*

§ 104. TABLE OF F-HOOK COMBINATIONS.

⟍ Pf or Pv	⟍ Bf Bv·	⎸ Tf Tv	⎸ Df Dv
⟋ CHf CHv	⟋ Jt Jv	⟋ Kf Kv	⟋ Gf Gv
⟋ Rf Rv	⟋ Hf Hv	⟋ wRf wRv	

§ 105. TABLE OF N-HOOK COMBINATIONS.

⟍ Pn	⟍ Bn	⟍ Tn	⟍ Dn	⟋ CHn	⟋ Jn
⟶ Kn	⟶ Gn	⟍ Fn	⟍ Vn	⟍ THn	⟍ Dhn
⟍ Sn	⟍ Zn	⟍ SHn	⟍ ZHn	⟍ Ln	⟍ Rn
⟍ Mn	⟍ Nn	⟍ NGn	⟍ Wn	⟍ Yn	⟍ MPn
⟍ Hn	⟍ wLn	⟍ wRn	⟍ wMn	⟍ wNn	⟍ Ru

§ 106. When N, F or V is the last consonant sound in a word
that ends with a vowel the stem sign must be used, as a hook
would indicate that the N, F or V was the final sound; thus,

⟍ *puff,*   ⟍ *puffy,*   ⟍ *pen,*   ⟍ *penny.*

§ 107. S or Z may be added to the *f*-hook and to the *n*-hook
on curves, by turning a small circle inside the hook; thus,
⟍ *puffs,* ⟍ *vanes.*

§ 108. On straight stems making the *n*-hook

1. Into a small circle adds   *s;* thus,   ⟍ *pens.*
2. "   " large   "   "   *ss;*   "   ⟍ *dunces.*
3. "   " small loop,   "   *st;*   "   ⟶ *against.*
4. "   " large   "   "   *str;*   "   ⟍ *punster.*

§ 109. The *n*-hook circles and loops must not be used in the
middle of words unless the hook and circle can be made distinct.

⁹ 110. S may be added to the *n*-hook circles and loops by
turning a *small* circle on the opposite side of the stem.

§ 111. Some students seem to think that because making the
n-hook on straight stems into a circle adds *s* that the same principle holds good when applied to that hook on curved stems and
the *f*-hook on straight stems. A little careful consideration will
show the fallacy of this, however, as should it be done the hook
would be lost and we would simply have the stem and added
s, instead of the *stem, hook* and *s.* The circle may be made a little
smaller than usual when written inside these hooks, so as not to
make the hooks too large. The *st*-loop or *large* circle is never
written inside these or any other hooks.

§ 112. In order to give a better form and to retain the primitive word the *f, v* or *n*-hook may be used in the middle of words

where convenient , but in words like *devices, devious* and *fence* the stems must be used, but in words like *puffery, bravery, gunnery, grainer, granary* the hooks should be employed; thus, $\curlyvee$ *bravery*, $\searrow_\circ$ *pennons*.

§ 113. *Have, of* or *ever* as a suffix, may be expressed by an *f*-hook on the preceding consonant stem, and *been* may be added to the *f*-hook on curved stems by turning a *small* hook inside it. The *f*-hook on curves must be made *longer* than on straight stems, and when the *n*-hook is turned inside the *v*-hook may be made a little larger than usual; thus, $\angle$ *which have no*, ℓ_o *they have been* $\ell_\frown$ *they may have been.*

§ 114. *Than, own, in* or *been* may be added by the *n*-hook; thus, $\frown$ *more than*, ∂ *there own*, λ *I have been*.

§ 115. F AND N-HOOK WORD SIGNS.

$\lvert$ differ-ence-ent,[3] $\diagup$ whichever,[2] $\frown$ govern,[2] $\sim_\smile$ opinion,[1] λ experience,[3] $\searrow$ phonography,[1] $($ within.[3]

READING EXERCISE No. 4.

KEY.

Line 1.—Puff, buff, tough, doff, chaff, cough, cave, jove, rough, raff, relief, grave, belief, prove, staff, stove.

Line 2.—Strive, pen, pawn, ten, chain, gain, gone, fan, fin, vain, stone, strain, spun, clan, main, than.

Line 3.—Man, men, woman, women, human, humane, earn, none, plain, shine, machine, flown, frown.

Line 4.—Cough, coffee, men, many, puffs, fines, pens, tenses, pounced, canister, punsters, ransom.

Line 5.—Fence, fences, devices, plain, plainer, mean, meaner, puffery, drive, driven, references, toughen.

Line 6.—All of, to all of, who have, should have, and of-have, they may have been, who have been, to have known, I have been, other than, larger than, which ever, live within your income.

Line 7.—There is no royal road to learning, success comes only by severe study and diligence. Out of his sight.

WRITING EXERCISE No. 6.

When *s*, *t* and *f*, or *s*, *t* and *v* are the only consonants in a word, and there is no vowel sound between the *s* and *t*, then use the *st*-loop and the stroke T; but when *s*, *t* and *n* are the only consonants in a word if the *n* is the final sound, use the *ess*-circle, stroke T and *n*-hook.

When the consonants *t* and *f*, *t* and *v*, *d* and *f*, or *d* and *v*, are immediately followed by *n*, the stroke T or D with the *f*-hook and stroke N must be used. Also when *d* or *t* is followed by *f* or *v* and *d* or *t* the stroke D or T with an *f*-hook must be employed.

WRITE IN ACCORDANCE WITH §§ 102–103.

Puff	pave	beef	tough	cuff
cough	cave	crave	grove	dove
chief	buff	proof	above	bluff
brief	trough	deprive	drive	drove
calf	clove	glove	aggrieve	stuff
stove	rough	belief	relief	scoff
strive	starve	roof	pen	pain
open	pin	plain	plan	been
boon	upon	happen	done	down
join	coin	queen	gone	again
gain	often	fan	fine	even
brain	brown	prune	thin	than
thine	then	shown	man	men
nine	mean	none	known	line
lone	lean	cane	run	roan

WRITE IN ACCORDANCE WITH §§ 106–107.

| men | many | purify | cough | coffee |
| cuffs | cloves | gloves | fines | mines |

WRITE IN ACCORDANCE WITH § 108.

happens	dense	prunes	brains	chance
plans	appliance	bronze	tense	chains
suspense	bounced	canister	against	appearances

WRITE IN ACCORDANCE WITH § 112.

puffery	gunnery	toughen	pennons	openness
plainer	private	profit	provide	prefer
defence	ignorance	grainer	franchise	chiefly
lonely	define	coffin	dinner	

SENTENCES.

Never say where ignorance is bliss 'tis folly to be wise.

Every man is free to express his opinion of the value of Phonography, in any *possible manner*.

. Scan closely the pages of any choice book, and *you will* gain wisdom.

The man drove *to* r *our* relief and before noon we were safe at home.

He who runs the fastest at first, *many times* loses the race.

There is no royal road to learning, success only comes by severe study and diligence.

Live within your income and *you will* owe *no man*.

Govern your desires before they govern you.

Place man in trying situations requiring nerve and courage and notice their different manners.

SHUN AND TER-HOOKS.

§ 116. When Phonography was in the early period of its existence only one size of final hooks was used, but careful experiment and daily practice showed that two sizes could be employed without endangering the legibility of the writing, and a large hook was taken to represent the frequently recurring sound of *shun*. On curved stems the hook is made on the *inner* side of the curve, a hook never being turned on the outer side, but on straight stems the hook was written on either the *n* or *f*-hook side, according to certain rules, giving two hooks for the representation of but one sound. This method of writing the hook on both side

of straight stems at length was seen to be a waste of Phonographic material and finally one author used a large hook on
the *n*-hook side for *-tive*, and one on the *f*-hook side for *shun*. But
for various Phonographic reasons and especially the advantage it
gives in phrase writing, the large hook on the *n*-hook side should
be used for the frequent recurring sounds of *ter*, *ther*, and *dher*.
The two Pitmans (Isaac and Benn), still retain the old method
of expressing *shun* by both large final hooks.

¿ 117. TABLE OF SHUN-HOOK COMBINATIONS.

Pshn	Bshn	Tshn	Dshn	CHshn
Jshn	Kshn	Gshn	Fshn	Vshn
THshn	DHshn	Sshn	Zshn	SHshn
ZHshn	Lshn	Rshn	Mshn	Nshn
NGshn	MPshn	Wshn	Yshn	Hshn
wMshn	wNshn	wLshn	wRshn	Rshn

¿ 118. When *sh* and *n* are the only consonants in a word, as in
ocean; when an accented vowel comes between the *sh* and *n*, as in
machine, then the stroke SH and *n*-hook must be used. In words
like *notion, mission, caution*, etc., the *shun*-hook should be used ·
thus, ⌐ *ocean*, ⌐ *machine*.

¿ 119. In words such as *accession, position, transition, physician*,
the sounds of *sesshun, sisshun*, are represented by continuing the
circle into a hook, and *s* is added to this hook by turning a small
circle inside it; thus, ⌐ *accession*, ⌐ *position*, ⌐ *transition*,
⌐ *physician*.

¿ 120. Like the *f* and *n*-hooks the *shun* and *esshon*-hook may be
used in the middle of words; thus, ⌐ *dictionary* ⌐ *transitional*.

¿ 121. SHUN-HOOK WORD SIGNS.

⌐ objection, ⌐ subjection, ⌐ signification, ⌐ formation,
⌐ information.

THE TER-HOOK.

§122. As has already been stated, a large final hook on the *n*-hook side of straight stems adds *ter*, *dher* or *ther*. This only applies to straight stems, as no *other* stem can take more than two final hooks, and a large hook on curved stems adds *shun*. The *ter*-hook is of great value to phonographers, yet the average student seldom at first gets a clear insight into its proper employment. When a word ends in the sound of *ter* this hook must not be used, when if the *ter* was omitted a complete word would be *left* as in *better, butter, chatter, patter*, but in such words as *bother, gather, clatter, character, collector, greater, cutter, gutter*, the hook may be used. It is true if the *ter* was omitted from the words *cutter, gutter*, a distinct word would be left, but as the *t* in such words is not written, but expressed in another way (by the halving principle not yet explained), and as *r* ending a word is generally written with the down stroke, the *ter*-hook must be added to *k* and *g* to express the added sylable *ter*. Also when the sound of *ter, dher* or *ther* follows *h* or *Ree* the *ter*-hook must be used.

§ 123. TABLE OF TER-HOOK COMBINATIONS.

Ptr   Btr   Ttr   Dtr   CHtr   Jtr

Ktr   Gtr   Rtr   Htr   wRtr

§ 124. The *ter*-hook may sometimes be used in the middle of words. The sound of *der* is never expressed by the *ter*-hook, but must be written with the stroke *D* and the *r*-hook; thus, *gather*, *reader*.

§ 125. *S* or *z* is added to the shun and ter hooks by turning a small circle inside the hooks; thus, *nations*, *gathers*. The *n*-hook may be written inside the *ter*-hook for the addition of the word *than*; thus, *rather than*.

§ 126. *Their, there*, or *they are*, is added to straight stems by the *ter*-hook; thus, *what they are*, *gave their*, *which they are*. This method of expressing the addition of these words is of great value in phrase writing and proves that in making the change from the *shun* to *ter* the student and advanced writer have been benefited both in the matter of speed and legibility.

READING EXERCISE No. 5.

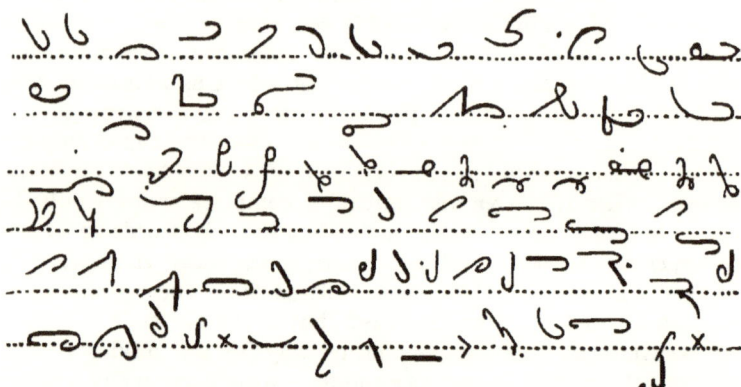

KEY.

Line 1.—Passion, fashion, motion, caution, ration, oration, ovation nation, national, lotion, fusion, section.

Line 2.—Sanction, ambition, attraction, selection, secretion, redemption, reception, distinction, affection.

Line 3.—Commission, relation, station, situation, position, possession, accession, transition, musician, imposition, succession, transitions, preposition.

Line 4.—Association, passionate, negotiation, cutter, gather, bother, hatter, character, collector, rather, glitter.

Line 5.—Writer, rioter, reader, greater, brother, motions, daughters, by their, at their, rather than, what they are, go there, can there be, come their way, had there been.

Line 6.—Greater than, we will be there, by their own, do all their. No objection should be given to the proper formation of the character of children.

WRITING EXERCISE No. 7.

WRITE IN ACCORDANCE WITH §§ 116-118.

passion	motion	caution	option	action
approbation	oration	ration	attribution	education
addition	duration	junction	excursion	commotion
commission	fashion	section	solution	collection
erasion	fusion	ovation	mission	nation

correction	collision	oppression	suppression	separation
discussion	deception	sanction	exhibition	suppression
solution	aggregation	ocean	situation	prevention
provision	prescription	subscription	permission	temptation
deviation	destination	discretion	duration	caption

WRITE IN ACCORDANCE WITH § 119.

| accession | possession | opposition | position | disposition |
| decision | accusation | succession | musician | sensation |

WRITE IN ACCORDANCE WITH § 120.

| rational | national | passionate | educational | additional |
| actionary | occasional | auctioneer | cautionary | stationary |

WRITE IN ACCORDANCE WITH § 122.

bother	tatter	rather	daughter	cutter
clatter	gutter	scatter	glitter	operator
carter	factor	captor	gather	character
collector	writer	heater	hatter	porter

WRITE IN ACCORDANCE WITH § 125.

| locations | passions | operations | portions | bothers |
| daughters | attractions | dimensions | caters | glitters |

SENTENCES.

No objection *should be* given *to the* proper formation *of the* character of children.

Man's subjection to temptation gives occasion, first, for dissipation, *and then* for reformation.

In this nation of *free men* every man may obtain office *if he can* secure enough influence.

Store your memory with valuable information, so when questions of importance arise *you may* assist *in the* elucidation.

Without opposition life becomes aimless and progression ceases.

It is necessary x *to* v *have* ambition to succeed *in this* life, because a man without ambition, *like a* ship *without a* rudder, is simply sailing to destruction.

Experience teaches us new ideas are unpopular with the masses of men, *and those* who *advance them must look* for opposition and persecution. What, then, *is the* duty of the reformer? *Shall he cease to proclaim his* message because men are unwilling to receive it? Nay. Pitying such ignorance he strives with more power to bring them higher and higher and nearer his level, till success finally crowns his endeavors.

LENGTHENING.

§ 127. As curved stems can take only *one* large final hook, and as such hook adds *shun*, the sounds of *ter, der, ther,* or *dher,* following such stems, excepting NG and MP-B, is expressed by making the stem twice its usual length. This lengthening principle is also used to add *their, there,* or *they are,* to curved stems (the same as the *ter*-hook does to straight stems), and to a straight stem, *providing it has a final hook,* and sometimes *other.* The addition of the latter word in this manner, however, can not receive a very high recommendation on account of the danger of its clashing with *their* and if it is so represented the short second place dash vowel must be written after the lengthened stem. Some phonographers also apply the lengthening principle to simple straight stems, but as the *ter*-hook represents the same additions it is not neccessary to lengthen straight stems to add *ter, dher,* or *ther.* A final hook is read before and a final circle or loop after the syllable added by the lengthening principle. In determining the position of lengthened stems regard the second half as a distinct sign, and write the first half in its proper position according to §§ 15–16; thus, ⟍ *senator,* ⟍ *whether,* ⟍ *on their,* ⟍ *of* or

have their, ⟍ *or they are,* ⟍ *may there,* ⟍ *mutters.*

§ 128. Sometimes in a sentence either of the syllables *ter, der, ther,* or *dher* is immediately followed by *their, there,* or *other,* and when this is the case the syllable and the word may be expressed by making the preceding consonant if curved three times its usual length.

§ 129. Doubling the length of NG adds *ker* or *ger* and of MP-B adds *er;* thus, ⟍ *banker,* ⟍ *younger,* ⟍ *temper,*

⟍ *timber.*

§ 129a. NG or MP-B may be lengthened, at times, to represent the sounds of *ter, der, ther* or *dher,* when there is no danger of such forms clashing with *ger, ker, mper* or *mber.* *There, their* or *they are* may be added by lengthening the NG or MP-B the same as any other curved stem.

READING EXERCISE No. 6.

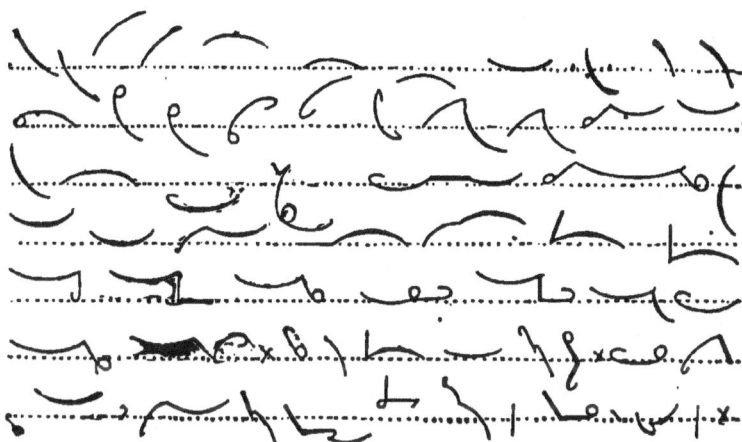

KEY.

Line 1.—Father, future, alter, letter, mitre, mother, metre, under, voter, order, water.

Line 2.—Smother, softer, sifter, cylinder, wilder, flounder, elevator, lifter, surrender, another.

Line 3.—Have their, may their, in order, I think there is no, we know they are going, surrender their places, with their.

Line 4.—Anger, younger, linger, cumber, lumber, jumper, timber.

Line 5.—Entertain, undertake, interpose, intersection, introduction, interview, we know they are.

Line 6.—Interposition, interpolation. Place your temper under proper subjection. We know there is, will there be.

Line 7.—The longer we linger before beginning a task the harder ·it becomes to finish it.

WRITING EXERCISE No. 8.

WRITE IN ACCORDANCE WITH § 127.

father	mother	enter	another
neither	latter	letter	order
matter	after	further	thither

loiter	lighter	metre	miter
smother	smoother	murder	winter
wonder	center	voter	weather
thunder	asunder	flounder	slender
matters	futures	undertake	entertain
interposition	interview	if there	for their
or their	in there	will there	offer there
of their	have their	over there	however there
think there	through their	the other	though there
was there	shall there	may their	some other
in there	no other	is in there	soon there
receive their	when there		

WRITE IN ACCORDANCE WITH ¿ 128.

further their	order their	murder their	whether there
enter their	center there	surrender their	render their

WRITE IN ACCORDANCE WITH ¿ 129.

anchor	anger	younger	longer
hunger	linger	sinker	rancor
anchorage	ember	temper	tamper
damper	chamber	lumber	jumper
bumpers	encumber	camper	timber

SENTENCES.

[A † before *their, there, they are,* or *other,* denotes that it is to be expressed by lengthening the preceding stem. The letters "wn" between two words indicates that the following word is expressed by the *w* and *n* hooks on the preceding stem.]

Sailors always *have* † *their* anchor ready, *so* † *there can be* no delay *when* † *there is necessity* for using it.

Place your temper under proper subjection.

No † *other person* can supply the place of father or mother.

Many boys and girls seem to *think* † *there is no necessity* x *for* † *their* acquiring an education, but without it they *can never become* anything but hewers of wood and drawers of water.

The longer we linger before *beginning a* x *task the* harder it becomes to finish it.

Without enterprise *no one* can hope to succeed in any business.

At wn *one time* x *it was necessary* x *for a* man to possess brains to become senator, now money *is the* substance which one *must have.*

Will the officials, *of* † *their* own free will, *surrender* † *their positions? Seeing* † *their* refusal *would be* foolish *they* l *will.*

HALVING.

§ 130. The sounds of *t* and *d* occur so frequently in words of daily use that it would seriously retard the speed of a phonographer were he compelled to write the full outlines, so in the early days of Phonography a shorter way of expressing these sounds was devised. It consists in writing the stem preceding the *t* or *d* one-half its usual length. This is called the halving principle, and takes effect on all stems except NG and MP-B, whether simple or compound. In adding *d* to N and M by the halving principle, they should be made heavy to distinguish from M*t* and N*t*. When *t* or *d* follows Ree or H, write both stems in full. Like the final hooks the *t* or *d* added by halving is read after the vowels and can be followed only by the *ess*-circle, therefore if a vowel sound follows the *t* or *d* the stroke stem must be used, so though *pit* would be written by a half length T, *pity* would be written with stroke P and T. A final hook is read before the added *t* or *d* and a final circle after; thus, ↘ pants, ↘ fashioned, ↘ *plants.*

§ 131. The positions of half-length stems are the same as full-lengths, with the exception of third place perpendicular and inclined, which are written immediately below the line; thus, ↘ *pat,* ⌐ *yet,* ⌐ *pit.*

§ 132. Half-length stems may be joined to other stems and used in the beginning, in the middle and the end of words; thus, ↘ *bottom,* ↘ *fortune,* ↘ *prevent.*

§ 133. Although half-length stems may be joined to other consonants, they must be distinguished by junction, length, width or curvature. K or G following F, V, or upward L; N or ING following P or B; F or V following D or T; or W following K or G, cannot be halved. Half-length K, F or V must not precede R or W; half-length P, B, T or D must not be joined to N or ING. Half-length N must not be joined to P, B, T or D. A half-length downward R following F, V, K or G must be thickened at the lower end. Two half-length straight stems written in the same direction should never be joined, as they could not be distinguished from single straight stems.

§ 134. When *ted* or *ded* follows another down stroke it is best to write a disjoined half-length D or T to keep the outline from extending too far below the line; thus, *date*, *dated*, *trade*, *traded*.

§ 135. When the sound of *est* follows the sound of *shun* immediately after K or G it may be represented by a half-length S written upward; thus, ⟍⟍ *factionist.*

§ 136. The past tense of words the present tense of which is expressed by a half-length stem, is written by the addition of the stroke D to the present.

§ 137. When *t* or *d* is the last consonant in a word that is followed by a vowel, or when it is immediately preceded by two vowels the stem sign should be used. The stem should also be used when the word ends in a circle or loop immediately preceded by a distinct vowel sound; thus, *pity,* *notice,* *poet,* *riot.*

§ 138. Half-length L when standing alone should be used to express the sounds of *lt* only, and when L is followed by *d* the stems must be used; but when joined to other stems half-length L may express either *lt* or *ld*; thus, *light,* *led.* *melt,* *mild.*

§ 139. When either *t* or *d* follows Ree the full outline should be used, to prevent any possibility of clashing with the ticks for *and* and *should,* but when joined to other stems half-length Ree may be used to express either the combination *r* and *t* or *r* and *d*; thus, *red,* *mart,* *mind,* *mired.*

§ 140. When final *d* is preceded by L, Ree or N, preceded and followed by a vowel, it should be written with the stroke D; thus, *solid,* *tarried,* *married.*

§ 141. *To* or *it* may be added to a word sign or preceding consonant by the halving principle; thus, *I am able to,* *by which it may be.*

§ 142. *Not* is added by the *n*-hook and halving principle combined; thus, *had not,* *do not,* *may not,* *it will not be.*

§ 143. HALF-LENGTH WORD SIGNS.

Particular,[1] opportunity,[2] ⁻according-to,[1] established-ment, movement.[3]

READING EXERCISE No. 7.

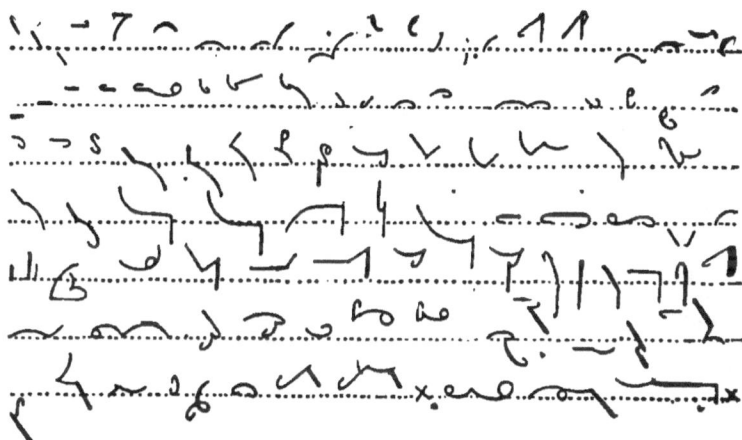

KEY.

Line 1.—Pat, paid, pit, cat, cattle, mat, met, metal, middle, fat, that, shut, sheet, let, hat, write, meet, made, nod, yet.

Line 2.—Good, get, God, glad, gladness, found, foundry, founder, paint, chained, meant, mind, moment, patient, stationed, sufficient, round.

Line. 3.—Around, count, plant, better, editor, chatter, standard, splendid, intent, part, fort, fortunate, appetite, prevent.

Line 4.—Patter, better than, fact, effect, looked, outfit, peanut, great, greater, sentiment, pete, cheat, late.

Line 5.—Date, dated, elocutionist, nicest, parted, cart, carted, enchant, enchanted, pretty, duty, beauty, kittie, druid, Hattie.

Line 6.—Merit, sometime, pensioned, mentioned, ancient, at all time, at all events, may not have been, cannot be, could not, be able to, according to, by which it might.

Line 7.—It will not be, shall not be, should not, they are not, this will not, we may not, we are able to, we are not able to. The sentences must not be neglected.

WRITING EXERCISE No. 9.

WRITE IN ACCORDANCE WITH § 130-131.

Pat	paid	jet	bought	bad
boat	beat	boot	cat	caught
cod	got	goat	get	good
chat	chewed	etched	aged	fat
food	act	thought	that	might
met	made	mad	mood	not
night	hand	end	light	let
art	put	added	void	vote
viewed	thanked	formed	used	shut
shoot	joined	happened	opened	broad
bred	bread	tried	child	joint
kind	account	called	acquaint	glad
gold	great	find	third	sent
send	sound	mind	amount	applied
pride	proud	proved	plant	spread
suspend	blood	brute	abroad	brought
bent	bend	blind	bound	blend
bland	told	toward	trade	attend
stand	sustained	stated	dreaded	cheered
comb	cared	sacred	gift	flood
short	bind	land	earned	around
rent	rend	round	surround	seemed
want	went	wound	signed	honored

WRITE IN ACCORDANCE WITH § 132.

Patter	chatter	better	editor	auditor
cattle	cotton	kitten	patron	matron
goodness	kindness	fondness	finder	foundry
paged	parted	shipped	pulled	boomed
reached	touched	jobbed	vouched	assumed
stripped	merit	malt	potatoes	potash
pottery	badly	actually	actual	greatly
actual	maturity	endless	little	ordinary
thoughtless	fortnight	fortunate	ascertained	abundant
gratified	esteemed	estimate	rectified	short-hand

WRITE IN ACCORDANCE WITH § 133-140.

fact	effect	vacate	looked	locked
peanuts	divide	bonnet	tuft	patent
correct	collect	deed	deeded	trust
treated	goaded	goal	act	acted
note	noted	vote	voted	beauty
plenty	mighty	led	led	lot
lawed	write	ride	treat	

SENTENCES.

[A"t" between two words indicates that the word following the t is expressed by halving the preceding stem; "n" that the following word is expressed by an *n*-hook on the preceding stem; "v" that the following word is expressed by a *v*-hook on the preceding stem. When *not*, with the preceding word, is enclosed by ‖ ‖ it indicates that the *not* is expressed by making the preceding stem half-length and adding an *n*-hook.]

You should be true to your friends *at* 1 *all* t *times.*

He who gave his honor *for a* moment's enjoyment *paid an* exhorbitant price.

The goods bought of you *the* † *other* day are almost worthless.

The halls of vice and palaces of sin may glitter, but behind *it* 1 *all* is degradation and despair; truly *all is not* gold that glitters.

The possession of great wealth *does not* always bring real enjoyment; the heart *of the* poor man is often more light and free than that *of the* millionaire.

Make *it a* point *to save* part of your income—no matter how small—for large fortunes *many times* x *have* n *been* formed through *such a* habit.

How often *when the* heart is bowed down *with a* weight of sorrow and affliction a word of cheer from some kind friend lifts the veil and penetrates the gloom, even *as the* morning sun dispels the darkness *of the* night.

Never judge *any one* without giving *him an* opportunity *to defend* himself.

[*We will*] *ship you* every fortnight, if [*we are*] *fortunate* in *obtaining the* required amount.

[*We may be*] *able* t *to* write short-hand; and yet if *we* ‖ *cannot* ‖ read what *we have* written *it* 1 *will be* of no benefit to us.

[*We may*] intend *to do* good, but if *we* ‖ *do not* ‖ carry *out* r *our* intentions *no one will be* benefited.

There are abundant opportunities for doing good on many occasions.

Why should we ask people *for* † *their* opinions when *we* ‖ *do not* ‖ intend *to respect them.*

There is a tide *in the* affairs of men which taken *at the* ebb leads on to fortune.

‖*Do not* ‖ mingle *in the* society *of the* wicked, for if we touch pitch *we* ‖ *can not* ‖ hope to escape being defiled.

Success comes only by hard labor and *there is no other* way *by which t it can be* obtained.

SIGN FOR REM.

§ 144. The rules previously given state that when *r* is the first consonant in a word and is preceded by a vowel it should be written with the down stroke, and when it is the first sound in the word Ree should be used, but before M the down stroke should be used whether preceded by a vowel or not. In a great many cases the observance of this rule results in the formation of long or awkward outlines, besides producing hesitancy in transcribing. To remedy this evil a sign is here given by which to represent this combination; thus, ⟋ Rem. "But," some one says, "that is H with an initial circle, and how are we going to distinguish one from the other?" The answer is simply this: There is no necessity for H taking an initial circle, as the only word given by any short-hand author where a vowel comes between the *s* and *h* and such combination could advantageously be used is *Soho*, and it would be folly to reserve a sign for just one word. But if it is desired to phrase *as he, has he,* or *is he*, it can be done by writing the *as, has* or *his* by the *ess*-circle and joining the tick for *he*. When a vowel comes before the *r* the *Rem* must not be used, nor when the *r* is *immediately* followed by two *m's*, nor when two vowel sounds are heard between the *r* and *m*, but in all other cases it may be employed; thus, ⟋⟍ *remove,* ⟋ *remain,* ⟍ *ramify,* ⟍ *has he[1],* ⟋ *roam.*

SIGN FOR YR.

§ 145. Y precedes *r* in a number of words where it must either be omitted or represented by the contracted *y*, which in phrase writing stands for *you*, and this makes the writing less legible. To obviate this difficulty the student may if he choose employ a large initial hook on Ree on the opposite side to the *w*-hook. This will not conflict with H if care is observed in the writing. This new form, like wR, will take all final modifications. In phrase writing it may be used for *you are*.

USE OF MP-B.

§ 146. The stroke MP-B must not be used when a vowel occurs between the *m* and *p* or *m* and *b*. When the sound of *m* is immediately followed by *p* or *b* then use this sign, but if the *p* or *b* is immediately followed by *r* or *l* and no distinct vowel sound is heard between the *p* and *r* or *l* or *b* and *r* or *l*, then the strokes M and P or B with an *r* or *l*-hook must be used. For an illustration take the word *empire*, which would be written with the stroke MP and Ree; *impose*, MP with an *ess*-circle; *improbable*, stroke M, stroke P with an *r*-hook and stroke B, *improb* being sufficient for legibility; *import*, MP with a half-length Ree; *employ*, stroke M and stroke P with an *l*-hook; *embellish*, strokes MB, L and SH.

PRIMITIVE AND DERIVATIVES.

§ 147. Generally when a student of Phonography becoming conversant with the modification of the consonant stems and the various expedients thus far explained, attempts to write words of any number of syllables, he is at a loss as to the proper form to employ, as apparently the word can be written with several forms each appearing proper and correct. The great fault of most Phonographic text books is that the style of writing they advocate is the commonly accepted theory of considering each portion of a word as an independent word and writing it with what appears to be the easiest and most flowing outline, irrespective of other words to which this particular one is related. Now the most philosophic way, and the one advocated in this work, is to consider every word as either primitive or derivative, and to write the derived outlines in accordance with the forms employed for their respective primitives; in other words to write the primitive word according to the general form and then add the additional consonants. If students, when beginning dictation practice will observe this rule, they will find much less trouble in writing and also in reading their notes when "cold." Take the words *grainer*, *granary*; their primitive is ⌒ *grain*, to write *grainer* the most philosophical way is to add the stroke R, ⌐ and for *granary* to add Ree, thus, ⌒. Examine the formation of the words, ꟾ *plant*, ⌐ *planter*, ⌐ *planning*, ⌐ *planting*.

∫ *plantation,* ⌐⋯ *plaintiff,* and ∖⌐∫⋅ *plainly,* all from the primitive ⌐ *play,* modified in the easiest and most natural manner. In the words *mean, meaner, meanest,* the primitive is ⋯⋯ *me,* adding an *n*-hook to that word and we have ⋯⋯ *mean,* adding R to *mean* and we have ⌐⋯ *meaner,* and *st* added to *mean* makes it *meanest,* but as an *st*-loop cannot be written inside a hook the *st* is added by a half-length S; thus, ⌐⊃ *meanest.* If to the outline, ⌐ *press,* we prefix an M, we have ⌐⋯ *impress;* a half-length N added to *press* gives us ⌐ *present;* if to *press* we add a stroke N with an *ess*-circle, it makes ⌐ *presence.* These few examples will give the student an insight into the application of this theory, and demonstrate that it may be used in the formation of all words—by first determining the natural way of writing the primitive and then adding the other syllables whether they precede or follow the primitive. The great benefit to be derived from this method of writing is that it renders outline writing more uniform and consistent, as it represents the language more faithfully and philosophically. By following this method students make more and easier progress and have much less difficulty in both taking and transcribing their notes—in the latter especially because the eye becoming accustomed to the primitive more readily deciphers the derivative. One of our rules for the formation of contractions, that of omitting the final strokes of a word that written in full would make a very extended outline, is based upon this theory.

§ 148. In writing some words according to this theory there may perhaps be a slight loss of speed, but the increase in legibility will more than balance it. This theory of form building has been too long overlooked, but it is destined in the near future to be adopted by all Phonographers and phonographic authors when its beauty and utility are more generally understood. The following will tend to help the student in this method of outline building: ⌐ *pay,* ⌐ *payment,* ⌐ *paymaster,* ⌐ *pond,* ⌐ *ponder,* ⌐ *ponderous,* ⌐ *pound,* ⌐ *pounder,* ⌐ *pounding, fie,* *find,* *finder,* *founder,* *foundry,* *foundation,* *men,* *mend,* *amendment,* *amending,* *standing,* *standard,* *stand by,* *understand,* *bet,* *better,* *man,* *manner,* *chair,* *chairman,* *fortune,* *unfortunate,* *tray,* *trade,* *trader,* *large,* *larger,* *largely,* *largest,* *for,* *forgot,* *forget,* *in,* *comes,* *incomes,* *pen,* *pension,* *continue,* *continued,* *continuation,* *merge,* *submerge,* *normal,* *abnormal,* *perfect,* *imperfect,* *person,* *personal.*

THE PAST TENSE.

§ 149. The past tense of a verb ending with a full length stem is indicated by halving such stem; thus, *blame,* *blamed;* when it ends with a half-length stem by adding the stem D. Verbs that end with the sound of *z* should be written in the past tense with the circle *s* and stroke D when only one stroke precedes, but by the *st*-loop after two or more strokes; thus, *cause,* *caused,* *gaze,* *gazed,* *refuse,* *refused.*

NS FOLLOWING A CURVE.

§ 150. When stroke N and circle *s*, following a curve, ends a noun in the the singular number, or a verb, write the stroke N, not the *n*-hook; thus, *fence,* *fences.*

READING EXERCISE No. 8.

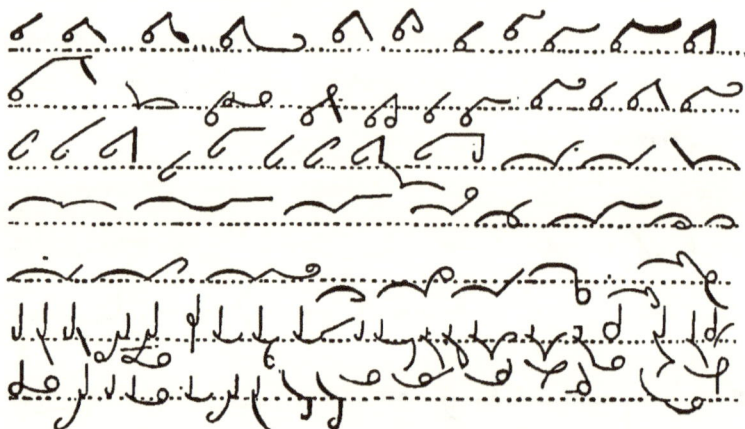

Line 1.—Ram, ramble, ramify, ramification, ramp, rampant, roam, remand, remain, remainder, remedy.

Line 2.—Remarkable, remember, reminiscence, remissible, remittance, room, ruminate, remnant, rum, rumble, rumination.

Line 3.—Yarn, yarrow, yard, year, york, yore, yearn, yardarm, Yorktown, empale, empire, bump.

Line 4.—Embalm, embank, embark, embarrass, embezzle, impaling, impatience, impatient.

Line 5.—Import, importer, impertinence, impugn, impulse, impure, impetus, imprint, impressive.

Line 6.—Ten, tenable, tenability, tenacious, tenaciousness, tenacity, tenant, tenantless, tenantry, tend, tendency, tender, tenderest, tenderloin, tenderly, tenderness, tense, tenfold, tenor, tensely.

Line 7.—Tenseness, tension, attend, attendance, attendant, attention, attentive, evident, evidence, nice, nicer, nicest, nicely, pounce, fence, nicety.

WRITING EXERCISE No. 10.

WRITE IN ACCORDANCE WITH ¿ 144.

Roam	room	rim	ram	rum
rumple	remainder	remnant	remotely	ramification

rampart	ream	remand	reminder	remission
rimple	romantic	ruminate	rumination	rumpus

WRITE IN ACCORDANCE WITH § 146.

Dump	lump	bump	ambition	ambush
amputate	champion	embezzle	embellish	embody
embrace	embolden	empale	embark	impair
impeach	impeachm'nt	impede	impelled	imperative
imperfect	impression	imperious	impersonate	impetuous
impetus	import	impose	impound	impoverish
impulse	impure	preemption	mop	mope

WRITE IN ACCORDANCE WITH § 147.

Ban	standard	actual	antecedence	anticlimax
band	standpoint	actually	antecedent	antidote
bandage	act	actuary	antechamber	antipathy
bandaging	acted	actuate	antedate	antique
bandbox	acting	ant	antepast	antiquary
stay	active	antagonize	antichrist	antiseptic
stand	actively	antagonism	anticipate	antithesis
standing	activity	antic	anticipation	antithetic

SENTENCES.

This is written to remind you that your remittance is not yet to hand. There now remains but one remedy.

We shipped you to-day the six reams Rome mill flat-cap, and *will ship* remainder *as soon as* you have room for it.

We shall remove to new and larger quarters, less remote *from the* business center, about the first of the month.

Embark in no enterprise that promises to impoverish anyone.

His first impulse was to impeach the testimony *of his* accuser.

The preemption laws *are not* fully understood.

Do not allow them to *remove their* last lot of goods until the bill is settled as per agreement?

When a steamer *from a* foreign country arrives in port the goods are taken in charge by the Custom House officials until the duties are paid *by the* importers.

We would call your attention to a special importation of ten cases of notions which we intend disposing of at remarkably low figures.

If you are not careful he will impose on you as he has imposed on others, for he *is an* imposter.

Success emboldens a man and impels him to renewed activity *in his* chosen profession.

CONTRACTIONS—PREFIXES AND SUFFIXES.

¿ 151. LIST OF PREFIXES.

1. Accom—By K disjoined, or joined if preferred; thus, *accommodate*, *accommodation*, *accomplish*.

2. Con, cum, com, cog—Either at the beginning or in the middle of words is represented by writing the part that follows the omitted syllable near the part that precedes it. At the beginning of a sentence, paragraph or line, the prefix may be indicated by writing a small dot near the beginning of the succeeding part of the word; thus, *they compose*, *recognize*, *condemn*.

3. Contra, contri, contro, or counter—By half-length K disjoined, or joined if preferred; thus, *controvert*, *contradict*, *contribution*, *counteract*, *contravened*, *countermand*, *countersign*.

4. For or fore—By F joined; thus, *forfeit*, *forever*, *forewarn*, *foretold*, *foremen*, *forehead*.

5. In—To words of the *sPr*-series and to *sM* and *sL* by the en-hook; thus, *in solitude*.

6. Intel—By a half length N; thus, *intellect*, *intellectually*.

7. Inter, intro, enter or under—By a double length N; thus, *intercession*, *interception*, *introduction*, *enterprise*, *entertain*, *understand*, *understood*.

8. Magna, magni, magne—By the stem M written over the first part of the remainder of the word; thus, *magnify*, *magnanimous*, *magnetism*.

9. Self—By an ess-circle written on the line; thus, *ᒐ *self* esteem.*

§ 152. LIST OF SUFFIXES.

1. Ble, bly—By the consonant B when it is inconvenient or impossible to use the stroke B with an *l*-hook; thus, ᑫ *sensible,* ᒪ *fashionable.*

2. For-f-m—By F joined; thus, ⟩ *therefore,* ⋀ *reform.*

3. Ing—By a light dot at the end of the preceding consonant, and *ings* by a small tick; thus, ⋰⋰ *patting,* ⋁ *pattings.* The *ing* dot and dash are used generally after contractions, stems with final loops and half length P, B and M.

4. Ility, ality, arity—Any consonant when disjoined from that which precedes it, expresses the addition of *ility, ality* or *arity,* or any other termination of similar sound; thus, ⟍ *penalty,* ⟋⟋ *regularity.*

5. Ly—When the L cannot conveniently be written upward to denote the *ly,* the L may be disjoined and written near the preceding part of the word or else written downward; thus, ⋎ *plainly.*

6. Mental, mentality—By a half length M with an *n*-hook written near the preceding part of the word; thus, ⌇ *instrumental;* the suffix may be joined when convenient without endangering the legibility.

7. Self—By a *small* circle joined to the preceding part of the word; thus, ⌐ *myself,* and *selves* by a *large* circle; thus, ⌊ᵒ *themselves,* ⟋ *ourselves.* When the signs for *self* or *selves* cannot be conveniently joined, it should be written beside the last stroke of the preceding part of the word; thus, ⟶ *man's self.*

8. Ship—By the stem SH joined or disjoined; thus, ⟩ *friendship,* ⟩ *lordship.*

9. SOEVER—By the stroke V with an initial circle joined to the preceding part of the word; thus, ⌇ *whensoever,* ⌇ *whencesoever,* ⌇ *whatsoever.*

§ 153. REGULAR PREFIXES.

"Regular Prefixes," so called to distinguish them from the prefixes expressed by some contracted form, are here given as a help in writing. The student should acquaint himself with the list so that he can write any of them without hesitation. If this is done speed will become easy of acquisition, as the student can spell the word phonetically in his mind and write it as he spells and yet take advantage of all the shortening principles. In the list the words are not illustrated by short-hand characters but by letters. Stems are represented by capital letters, and the various modifications by lower case italics. The small circle, large circle, *st-* and *str*-loops by *s, ss, st,* and *str* respectively; the *l, r, f, n, shun,* and *ter* hooks by *l, r, f, n, shn,* and *tr* respectively; the *isshun*-hook by SHN in small caps; the in-hook by a small cap N; the lengthening principle by *tr;* the halving principle by *t* or *d;* and an *n*-hook turned inside any other hook by a small cap N; a capital italic letter indicates that the consonant is to be written upward; a : indicates that the stems are to be joined; a superior ^{1}, ^{2}, or ^{3}, after a stem indicates that its position is first, second or third place, according as it is ^{1}, ^{2}, ^{3}.

LIST.

The prefixes are grouped, that is all the prefixes represented by the same form are given together.

AB, BE, BI, BY, OB—By B; thus, B²:*Jshn, objection,* B¹:*sL*:V, *absolve;* B²:T*r, betray,* B³:G:M, *bigamy,* B¹:W, *byway.*

AC, CO, EC, OC—By K; thus, K:*s*D³, *accede,* K:P¹*rt, co-operate,* K*s*: T¹*t*:K, *ecstatic,* K:P¹, *occupy.*

AF, EF, OF, FORE—By F; thus, F³:N:T, *affinity,* F²:K:T, *effect,* F¹*s*: R, *officer,* F²:B*d, fore-bode.*

AFTER—By F*tr;* thus, F¹*tr*:N*n, afternoon,* F¹*tr*:wR*ds, afterwards.*

AG, IG—By G; thus, G*r:*V¹*t, aggravate,* G¹:N*t, ignite.*

. AL, IL—By L; thus, L³:D, *allude,* L³*s*:T*rt, illustrate.*

AMB, EMB—By MB; thus, MB³:G*s, ambiguous,* MB:G:T⁸, *ambiguity,* MB:*L*³:SH, *embellish,* MB:*R*¹:K, *embark.*

AMPHI—By M:F ; thus, M:F :B*s*, *amphibious.*

AN, ANA, EN, IN, UN, UNI—By N; thus, N:B¹:P, *ana-baptist.* N:Kr:
J², *encourage,* N:D³d, *indeed,* N:V²r*s:L, universally.*

ANT, ANTE, ANTI—By N*t;* thus, N*t*:R¹:K:T:K, *antartic,* N*t:s*D'*nt,*
antecedent, N*t*¹:K*rst, anti-christ.*

AP, EPI, OP, UP—By P; thus, P¹:T*t, appetite,* P²:D:M:K, *epidemic,*
P¹:R, *opera,* P²:*s*T, *upset.*

ARCH—By R:CH, or R:K, according as the sound is *arch* or
ark; thus, R¹:CH:D:K, *arch-duke,* R¹:K:T:K*t, architect.*

AS, ES—By S ; thus, S³*st, assist,* S²:Tr, *estray.*

ASTRO—By S*tr;* thus, S¹*tr*:N:M, *astronomy.*

AUTO, OUT, AT—By T ; thus, T¹:K*rt, autocrat,* T¹:*s*D, *outside,* T²:
M*t, attempt.*

BEN, BENE—By B*n;* thus, B²*n:*F*t, benefit,* B²n:V:L*nt, benevolent.*

BIS—By B*s;* thus, B³*s:*K*t, biscuit,* B*s*²:T*n, abstain.*

CAL, COL—By K*l;* thus, K*l*¹:K*lt, calculate,* K*lf:*R¹:N, *California,*
K²*l:*K*tr, collector,* K*l:*J¹, *college.*

CAT, CATA—By K*t;* thus, K*t:L*¹, *cattle,* K*t:L*¹:G, *catalogue.*

CATE—By K:T; thus, K:T¹:K:*s*M, *catechism,* K:T¹:G:R, *category.*

CATER—By K*tr;* thus, K*tr*:R², *caterer.*

CENT, CENTU, CENTI, SEND, SENT—By *s*N*t;* thus, *s*N*t*:R², *centenary,*
*s*N²*t:*Gr:M, *centigram,* *s*N²*d:*NG, *sending,* *s*N²*t:*M*nt, sentiment.*

CHRON—By K*rn;* thus, K¹*rn:*K, *chronic,* K*rn:L*¹:J, *chronology.*

CIR, SER, SUR—By *s*R if it is followed by a horizontal or upstroke, but *s*R if the next stroke is perpendicular or inclined;
thus, *s*R²:K*s, circus,* *s*R²:P*nt, serpent,* *s*R¹:M*nt, surmount,* *s*R²:J, *surge,*
*s*R²:L, *surly,* *s*R²:P*ls, surplus,* *s*R²:K*l, circle.*

CIS, SYS—By *ss;* thus, *ss*T²*rn, cistern,* *ss*T¹³:M, *system.*

COR, CUR, CAR—By K*r;* thus, K*rs:*P¹*nd, correspond,* K*r:*N:S₂, *cur-
rency,* K*rd:*L², *curdle,* K²*rt:*N, *curtain,* K*r:*B¹*n, carbon.*

COSMO—By K:*s*M ; thus, K:*s*M:P¹*l:*T*n, cosmopolitan.*

DE, DI, DIA, DU, DUO, AD—By D; thus, D¹:P*s, depose,* D¹:M*tr, dia-
meter,* D²:L*st, dullest,* D²:D:*s*M, *duodecimo,* D¹:K*wt, adequate.*

DEC—By D:K; thus, D¹:K:MP, *decamp,* D²:K*tr, Decatur.*

DEF, DEV, DIF—By D*f* or D:F; thus, D*f*²:N*s, defense,* D¹*f:*D*nt,*
diffident, D³:V*s, devious,* when the *f* is immediately followed by *n*
or *t* or *d* use the D*f.*

DES, DIS, DYS—By D*s;* thus, D²*s:*P:R, *despair,* D²*s:*K*v:*R, *discovery,*
D²*s:*P:P, *dyspepsia.*

DEST, DIST—By D*st;* thus, D²*st:*N, *destiny,* D³*st:*NG*t, distinct,* D²*tr:*
B, *disturb,* D³*str:*K*t, district.*

EM, IM—By M; thus, M²:N:N*t*, *eminent*, M:P³*l*:K*t*, *implicate*.

EX—By K*s*; thus, K:*s*R²*ss*, *exercise*, K²*s*:K*l*:M, *exclaim*, K*s*:P*ins*, *expanse*.

EQUI—By K*w*; thus, K*w*:P²:J, *equipage*, K*w*:D³*st*:N*t*, *equi-distant*.

GEO—By J; thus, J*ı*:M:T*r*, *geometry*.

HEX—By *h*K*s*; thus, *h*K²*s*:G*n*, *hexagon*.

IR, ER—By R or *R*; thus, R*s*:G*t*, *irrigate*, R³:T*t*, *irritate*, R²:V*rnt*, *irreverent*, R²:R, *error*, R²:P*shn*, *eruption*.

LITH—By *L*:TH; thus *L*ʌ:TH:G*rf*, *lithograph*.

MAL, MEL, MIL—By M:*L*; thus, M:*L*¹*s*, *malice*, M:*L*²:D, *melody*, M: *L*³:R, *miller*.

MANU, MONO, OMNI—By M:N; thus, M:N:P¹:*Lt*, *manipulate*, M:N: L¹, *manual*, M:N:P¹:*Ls*, *monopolize*, M:N:P³:T*nt*, *omnipotent*.

MED, META, METE—By M*t*; thus, M²*d*:K*l*, *medical*, M*t*:F³*s*:K, *metaphysic*, M*t*:*L*¹:K, *metallic*.

MULT—By M:*Lt*; thus, M:*L*²*t*:P*l*, *multiply*, M:*L*²*t*:T*d*, *multitude*.

MYTH—By M:TH; thus, M:TH³:K*l* *mythical*.

NON—By N*n*, when convenient, or N:N; thus, N*n*:R²*s*:D*nt*, *nonresident*, N:N:N:T²:T, *nonentity*.

OVER, EVER, EVERY—By V*r*; thus, V²*r*:K, *overcome*, V²*r*:G*rn*, *evergreen*, V²*r*:wR, *everywhere*, V²*rn*, *every one*.

PAN—By P*n*; thus, P¹*n*:K:K, *pan-cake*, P¹*n*:Z, *pansy*, P¹:N*r*:M, *panorama*, P¹*n*:T:*Ln*, *pantaloon*, P¹:N:TH*r*, *panther*.

PER—By P:R, but sometimes by P*r*; thus, P²:R:*s*N, *person*, P³*r*: *ss*T, *persist*, P²*rs*:wD, *persuade*, P¹*r*:P*s*, *perhaps*.

PHIL, FULL—By F*l*; thus, F²*l*:D*l*, *Philadelphia*, F²*l*:F*l*, *fulfill*.

PLEN—By P*ln*; thus, P²*ln*:T, *plenty*.

PRIM—By P*r*:M; thus, P²*r*:M:R*s*, *primrose*, P¹*r*:M:R, *primary*.

PRO—By P*r*; thus, P¹*r*:V*d*, *provide*, P¹*r*:F*t*, *profit*, P¹*r*:P:R:T, *property*.

. PROTO—By P*rt*; thus, P²*rt*:T:P, *prototype*.

QUAD—By K*wd*; thus, K*wd*:R*int*, *quadrant*, K*wd*:R*itr*, *quadrature*.

RAM, REM, RIM, RUM—By R*m*; thus, R*m*¹:P*nt*, *rampant*, R*m³n*:*s*N*s*, *reminiscense*, R*m*²:B*l*, *rumble*.

. RE—By *R*; thus, *R*³:SH*r*, *reassure*, *R*³:B:K, *rebuke*.

REAL—By R*l*; thus, R*l*¹:T, *reality*, *R*³*ls*, *realize*.

RETRO—By R*t*; thus, R²*t*:*s*P:K*t*, *retrospect*.

SEX—By *s*K*s*; thus, *s*K*s*:T²*n*, *sexton*.

. SEL, SOL, CEL—By *s*L; thus, *s*L³:D:F, *solidify*, *s*L³:D*f*:D, *solidified*, *s*L³:D:M, *seldom*, *s*L²:K*shn*, *selection*, *s*L²:R, *cellar*.

SUB—By sB; thus, sB^{2}s:Tn, *substantiation*, sB^3:Ms:V, *submissive*, sB^2:sL, *subsoil*.

SUPER, SUPRA—By sPr; thus, sP^{3}r:N:Ds, *superinduce*, sP^{7}r:M:S, *supremacy*.

TRANS—By Trns; thus, T^{1}rns:T, *transit*, sometimes the n can be omitted, T^{1}rs:Kshn, *transaction*, T^{1}rs:Kr:Pt, *transcript*.

TRI, UTTER—By Tr; thus, T^{1}r:M:F, *triumph*, T^{1}r:L, *trial*, T^{2}r:L, *utterly*.

WITH—By DH; thus, DH^1:Dr, *withdraw*, DH^{3}n, *within*.

OMISSION OF CONSONANTS.

§ 154. The following consonants may be omitted:

1. K or G after NG, unless the K or G is final; thus, ⌣ *sanction*, ⌐ *distinctions*, ⌣ *angle*[1].

2. T between s and another consonant; thus, ＼ *postpaid*.

3. P between T and another consonant; if no vowel follows; thus, ⌐ *tempt*, ⌐ *dumped*.

4. N before the sound of *jer*; thus, ⟩ *passenger*[1], ⌐⟩ *messenger*.

5. K from such words as *construction*, *refraction*, *restriction*; thus, ℒ *instruction*, ⟋ *refractioni*.

6. N from such words as *transpose*, *attainment*, *transgress*, etc.; thus, ⟍ *transpose*, ⌐ *atonement*.

7. L between the strokes N and J; thus, ⟋ *knowledge*[1], ⟍ *intelligent*, ⟋ *intelligence*.

8. Words ending in *-ntial* or *-ntially*, may be abbreviated by leaving off the final syllable, *-tial* or *-tially*; thus, ⌐ *financial*[1], ⟩ *substantiali*, ⟍ *confidentially*.

OMISSION OF WORDS.

§ 155. The following words may be omitted:

1. OF—Between two nouns which can be joined to denote the omission.

2. AND—From the middle of a phrase and the adjacent words joined; thus, ⌒ *more and more.*

3. OR—From such phrases as ⌒ *more or less.*

4. To—From such phrases as ‾ *according to* ⌐ *in respect to,* ⌐ *in regard to.*

5. FROM- TO—From such phrases as || *from day to day,* ⟍

from hour to hour.

WRITING EXERCISE No. 11.

WRITE IN ACCORDANCE WITH ¿ 151.

Accompany	foreclose	contraband	accomplishment
they compare	foregone	controversy	condensation
incomplete	introduce	counteractive	maganimous
comprehensive	accomplice	forefather	selfevident
magnify	no comparison	undertake	counterpart
selfish	they combine	interrupt	counterbalance
self-interest	condition	recognize	foremost
contravene	magnetism	recompense	interview
counterpoise	self-esteem	contradistinction	

WRITE IN ACCORDANCE WITH ¿ 152.

Sensible	itself	popularity	pleadings
bleeding	wheresoever	fundamental	instability
meetings	fashionable	township	detrimental
plainly	arresting	patting	lordship

WRITE IN ACCORDANCE WITH ¿ 154.

Anxiety	transcribe	tempt	mostly
function	providential	transpose	passenger
lastly	anxious	financial	transport
refraction	testimony	junction	essential

WRITE IN ACCORDANCE WITH ¿ 155.

Gentlemen of the jury	bill of lading	last will and testament
ladies and gentlemen	less and less	breach of promise
from time to time	mean to be	for ever and ever
in point of fact	bill of sale	more and more
we mean to have	more or less	in regard to
from place to place	one or both	from day to day

SENTENCES.

The convention then resolved itself into a committee of the whole.

Neither despise nor oppose what you *do not* understanu.

Ample compensation *will be* allowed *if you* undertake the task and successfully complete it.

Our goods *are all* in first-class condition and the prices compare favorably with any ever given.

Beware of any person whose only recommendation is that of personal magnetism.

Self-esteem *is not* pernicious, *but the* egotistical man soon becomes an object of ridicule and is despised by all sensible people.

Education *is the* fundamental principle of civilization.

Gold and silver money is more easily counterfeited than paper.

Never undertake to applaud *your own* virtues or present your good deeds for approval; let *some* n *one* else interpose a few good words in your behalf *if you* desire popularity.

(*We will be*) *pleased* x *to mail* you *from time to time*, or with regularity *if you* desire, plainly printed quotations of the market.

The experience you have gained will *more* n *than* counterbalance any financial loss *you may* v *have* sustained.

A duplicate bill of lading *has been* sent.

Never contradict or interrupt *any one*.

In r † *order that we may be able to* meet our obligations your bill *must be* paid *at* wns *once.*

REMARKS ON PHRASE WRITING.

¿ 156. A proper and judicious use of phraseography (joining words together occurring in phrases and clauses) is one of the greatest aids to rapid writing. The forms thus given are more compact, and will, in all probability, be more carefully written as they require less time, and therefore will be more easily read. It is possible to join the words together in such a manner as to make the phrase almost unintelligible. No time is saved in writing awkward combinations, as transcribing becomes a mere matter of guess-work and therefore incorrect. Such phrases as, "which-they-would," "shall-you-be," "do-you-have," "with-us," "will-you-have," etc., are forms that retard rather than facilitate speed, and are very hard to decipher.

¿ 157. Phrases should consist of words that are naturally collected in meaning, such as pronouns and verbs, prepositions and pronouns, adjectives and nouns, several verbs, and words that are naturally connected in a phrase or clause; thus, "as-well-as," "as-well-as-can-be," "you-may." "by-their," "great-men," "may-have-been," "I-am-as-well-as-usual," but there should be no straining after phrases. They may be composed entirely of contracted words, or of words that are not contracted, or of contracted or uncontracted words.

§ 158. The *first* word of a phrase should be written in its proper position with respect to the line of writing, the other words being joined to the first without respect to their proper position. But when the first word of the phrase belongs to the first position, and is represented by a circle, loop or horizontal stem, or any half-length stem, if necessary to secure greater legibility, the first word may be raised or lowered so as to allow the second word of the phrase to be written in the position it would occupy if standing alone.

§ 159. CAUTION.

1. Words which are not united in phrases or clauses must not be joined.

2. Words whose junction would be awkward, or not allowable, must not be joined.

3. No phraseogram should extend more than two strokes below the line.

4. Phraseograms of inconvenient length should not be employed. More than ten words should never be joined.

5. *At least* must be written ⌡ to distinguish it from ⌐ *at last*. *No, go, own, least, else, see, ill,* when joined to the preceding word should be vocalized to distinguish them from *any, come, know, last, less, say, well.* When *change* is thrown out of position, write it in full to distinguish it from *charge; gentleman* should be written J¹nt to distinguish it from J²nt *gentlemen. Inner* should always be vocalized to distinguish it from *near* and *leave* to prevent its conflicting with *live. Ever* as a word sign, whether standing alone or used in phrases, should always be written V²r, but as a suffix it may be written with the *v*-hook.

§ 160. The leading principles governing the formation of phrases have now been explained. There is scarcely any limit to the extent to which they can be used. On the following two pages will be found a list of very useful ones which should be carefully studied.

Able to think
absolutely necessary
according to
act of Congress
after that time
again and again
and has been
any one
as far as
as fast as
as long as
as it
as it is
at once
at or about that time
at the present time
at their own
before there
better than
by all means
by their own
by which it may be
by which there
Can there be
can there not be
could not be
debenture bond
do not be
do their part
do you mean to say
did all their
Every consideration
financial agents
for my part
for there has been
Give there
greater than
Had been
had there been
have all
have been there
has not earned
he could not have been
he would not have been
I am glad
I am sure
I do not think
I have been
I hope you will be
I know there has been
I may not be
I think there is
I will not be
in order that we may be
in relation to
is it not
it is important
it is impossible
it is well known
it would have been

Just as well as
just been
Let us be
less than
lower rates
Most likely
must have been
must not be
my dear brother
my dear sir
No such thing
Of course it is
on account of
ought not to have
ought not to be
Railroad company
railroad station
railway company
rather be
rather have
rather than
Sec. of State
seems to be
shall be
shall not be
shall our
shall our own
so there may be
some one
such has been
such have been
That has been
that it may be
that the company
that the payment
there has been
they have not been
they will have
We are able to
we are not able to
we are ready
we did not
we do not
we have been
we may be able to
we may have been
we may not be
we will be there
we will not be
we will ship
when there has been
what was the matter
which will be
with which they are
would have been
You are
you are not
you have been
you will not
your own

RULES FOR FORMING CONTRACTIONS.

§ 161. The following rules will enable the student to intelligently abbreviate words that written in full would present too extended outlines:

1. ABSTRACT—may be indicated by writing the stem B through the following perpendicular or horizontal stem; thus, ⌐ *abstract clerk.*

2. AGENT—by an intersected J; thus, ⊁ *insurance agent.*

3. ASSOCIATION—by an intersected SH; thus, ✗ *Building Association.*

4. COMPANY—by an intersected K; thus, ⌐ *joint stock company.*

5. DEPARTMENT—by an intersected D; thus, ⟍ *abstract department,* ⊢⌐ *claim department.*

6. DIRECTOR—by an intersected Dr; thus, ⊰ *new director.*

7. MANAGER—by an intersected M; thus, ⟋⊸ *manager's office.*

8. OFFICIAL—by an intersected F; thus, ⊰ *government official.*

9. RAILROAD—by an intersected Ree; thus, ✗ *Pennsylvania Railroad,* ⟋ *railroad manager, railway* by Rl intersected.

10. SOCIETY—by an intersected S; thus, ⫽ *law society.*

11. SUPERINTENDENT—by an intersected sPr; thus, ✗ *general superintendent,* ⟍ *superintendent's department.*

The principle of intersected letters standing for words may be applied further than according to the rules given here, as in any special branch of short-hand work one or more words may be very frequently employed and these may be represented by striking the principal consonant through the other word. Thus in the railroad business the word *passenger* might occur very frequently and this could be represented by an intersected P; in law reporting *plaintiff* might occur very frequently and could be indicated by an intersected P.

12. CON may be omitted from the middle of words, and sometimes initially; thus, ⌐ *inconsistent,* ⌐ *combined.*

13. Omit K from such syllables as *-action, -ection*, etc.

14. Omit *circum* from such words as *circumscribe, circumstance*, etc.

15. Omit N from words of more than three strokes.

16. Omit the final syllables, *-tial, -tially*.

17. Generally when a word that written in full would extend to more than three strokes omit the latter part.

18. The final syllable *ments* may be written M*ts*.

19. The common long-hand abbreviations may also be used as contractions in short-hand writing; thus, J¹:N, *January,* J¹*nt, gentleman,* J²*n, general-ly,* D²:M, *democrat-ic,* D¹:M:K, *democracy, s*G³, *signify-icant,* N:Y¹, *New York,* J³*r, junior,* M:N:F¹, *manufacturer,* K:P¹, *captain,* D¹*r, doctor,* D²*r, debtor,* R:J³, *original,* N³*s, insurance,* R²:G, *regular,* B²*rn, brethren,* R²*s*:G, *resignation.*

WORD SIGNS OR GRAMMALOGUES.

§ 162. In every work on short-hand heretofore published will be found a long list of "grammalogues" or "word signs," which the student is told must be learned before dictation can begin. This is a stupendous task and one over which the student generally becomes discouraged, and is the cause of so many failing to acquire this science. A careful analysis of these lists will generally show that nearly seventy-five per cent. of the words therein contained are not represented by arbitrary signs but are simply written in the reporting style, while the remainder are represented by some suggestive sign. The knowledge of this fact would save the student seventy-five per cent. of the time required to memorize the entire list, and this time put into practicing from dictation would enable him sooner to acquire the speed sought.

§ 163. This knowledge has been used in the compilation of the word signs given in this work, and instead of a list of 427, as in Isaac Pitman's Manual and "Reporters' Companion," from which the most of these are taken, only 75 are presented to be memorized. This list contains a number not given in Pitman's, so the real reduction is nearly eighty-five per cent. The student has already had in his writing exercises all the "grammalogues" not given in this list, so he has become familiar with them without any usual study or exertion.

HOW IT IS ACCOMPLISHED.

This reduction is accomplished by writing the 80 per cent. not

here given, in the regular "Reporting Style." This simply consists of taking advantage of every shortening principle, omitting
all vowels and writing the outline in position when standing
alone, or when joined in phrases by writing the first word in the
position it would occupy if standing alone. To illustrate, take
the word *happy*, $\searrow$ given as a grammalogue by Pitman, would in
the reporting style be written P¹, because the accent is on the
first syllable, and *h* before P is omitted; *proof*, would be so
written in the reporting style because *r* would be added by the
r and *f* by the *f*-hook, and the vowel is third place; *mine* is written because *i* is first place and *n* final is represented by the
n-hook; *mind* because *d* is added by the halving principle;
myself, because the *ess*-circle is used to express the addition
of *self*; *matter*, by Mdr in the first position, because the
sound of *ter, der, dhr* or *ther*, may be added to any curved stem by
lengthening, and the vowel is first place; *they are*, $)$ because
they would be written (and *are* is added by the *r*-hook; *more*,
written so, although there is a distinct vowel sound between
the *m* and *r*, because there is no danger of its conflicting with
any other word and is a brief way of writing a frequently occurring word. These few illustrations will show the principle
employed in the reduction of this list, and how much time has
been saved the student in consequence.

§ 164. The following is a list of all the arbitrary "word signs" in
Isaac Pitman's list and a few which it has been thought best to
add. It will be noticed that these signs are generally the principal consonant of the word and are written in the position of the
accented vowel except for *go*, so written to prevent its conflicting with come, in case the G was made too light or the K
too heavy; / in second position for *which* to prevent its conflicting with CH in third position for *each*; and *any* to prevent conflicting with *no*; in a phrase *no* should always be
vocalized.

§ 165. LIST OF WORD-SIGNS.

*A, all, an		movement, never, next	
and			
any		number, opinion, opportunity	
advantage			
are, as, as-his-is		object, objection, *part	
as has, beyond, but		particular, phonography, principal	
can, change, charge		principle, remember, satisfactory	
come, could, do, defendant		somewhat, special, *strength	
*differ, *difference, *different		*strong, several, shall	
especial-ly, first, form		should, *signify, similar	
gave, give-n, go		similarity, thank, think	
has, has his-is, how		thing, time, to, two	
*however, important, importance		truth, usual, what	
*impossible, improve, improved		which, who, will	
influence, language, large		would, young, *youth	
long, length, member			

Words marked (*) are not "grammalogues," but either the forms written in accordance with the regular reporting style or else the contracted slang expressions so frequently used.

CONTRACTIONS.

§ 166. What has been said of large lists of word signs also applies to "contractions," and no rules have heretofore been given for their formation. By the application of the rules previously given the labor of memorizing a large list is avoided, and more time saved the student for practice, without any loss of speed.

Take the contraction ∫ *circumstantially*, reference to the rules will show that *circum* may be omitted, and when a word ends in *-tially* that syllable may be omitted; ∫ *development*, by the rule that when a word would extend to more than three strokes if written in full omit the latter part; ⌐⁄ *knowledge,* by the rule that *l* between *n* and *j* should be omitted.

§ 167. The following list contains a number of contractions which in other works would be given as arbitrary and to be memorized. They are all formed, however, according to previous rules, and given here simply to assist the student in the formation of other contractions; they need *not* be memorized but should be written several times until the principles involved in their construction is understood.

LIST.

Advertise, D_1
advertisement, D^l
baptist, B^l:P
baptised, B^l:P
baptism, B^l:P
because, K_1s,
benevolent, B^2n:V
business, B^3s
cabinet, K_1:B
Catholic, K_1:TH
catholicism, K^l:TH
certain, sR^2t
certainly, sR^2t
develop-ed, D^2:Vl
development, D^2:Vl
derogatory, D^lr:G
difficult, D^3f:K
dignify, D^3:G
dignity, D^3:G
disadvantage, D_{2s}:J
document, D^l:K
enthusiasm, N:TH^3s
equivalent, K^3wv
excuse, sK^3s
exhorbitance, G:sR^l:B
exhorbitant, G:sR^l:B
exhorbitantly, G:sR^l:B
expect, sP^2:Kt
expensive, Ks:P^2ns
expensiveness, Ks:P^2ns
extraordinary, K:sT^lr:Rd
extravagance, K:sT^lrv
facility, F^3s:L
February, F^2:B

federal, F_2:D
gentlemen, J^2nt
generalize, J^2ns
generalization, J^2nsSHN
governor, G:V^2
immediately, Ms:Md
impracticable, M:P^lr:K
improbable, M:P^lr:B
incapable, N:K:P$_2$
indignant, Nsd:G
insignificant, N^3s:G
irregular, R^2:G
magazine, M$_1$:G
mechanical, M^l:Kn
Mr, M^3r
northwest, Nr:W^1st
November, N:V^2
practical, Pv:K
preliminary, P^3r:L:M
prerogative, P^lr:R:G
public, P^4:B
publish, P$_2$:B
republic, R^2:P:B
republican, R^2:P:B
represent, R^l:P
representative, R^2:P
repugnant, R^2:P:G
responsible, R^ls:Pns
reverend, R^2:V
revenue, R^2:V
signature, sG^3
signify, sG^3
surprise, sP^lrs
temperance, T^2:MP

INITIALS.

§ 168. Initials should be expressed in long hand whenever the speed of the speaker is not too great to permit, but sometimes it is necessary to express them phonographically. Most phonographic authors say that C and Q should be written in long hand and that G should be expressed by the consonant G. The best way of expressing Q is by the consonant K with the w-hook ⌣ , C by the consonant) in the *third* position, and G by the stroke / in the *third* position. If this is done G and J and S and C will never conflict, as J should be represented by the stroke / in the *second* position, and S by the stroke) in the *second* position. R should be represented by Ree and W by the stroke W; the object in writing Ree for the initial R is to prevent W and R ever conflicting. Y should be represented by the contracted Y opening upward; if this is done Y and L will never conflict. P, T, and V should be represented by the corresponding consonants written in the *third* position, and B, D, and F by the corresponding consonants written in the *second* position. A is represented by a *heavy dot* in the *second* position (on the line) and E by a *heavy dot* just *below* the line, I by ∨, U by ⌢, and O by the word sign for *awe*. Z should be represented by a small circle in the *third* position.

EXPRESSION OF NUMBERS.

§ 169. Whenever possible, figures should be expressed by the ordinary Arabic characters. While in some instances they are not as. brief as the words phonographically written, they are somewhat more legible, and their distinctive character renders them conspicuous in the midst of the general writing and is of advantage when the notes have often to be referred to. It is best, however, always. to write *one* and *ten* in short-hand. When several ciphers occur the number represented by them should be expressed in phonography; thus, 27 ⌣ *27,000*, 80 ⌣ *80,000,000*, ⌡ 8, *10,008*. In rapid reporting the following short-hand letters, written close to the figures, will be found useful : ⌣ *hundred*, (*thousand*, ⌢

million, ⌐{ *hundred thousand,* ⌐⌐ *hundred million,* \ *billion.*

Dollars should be written at the end of the number; thus, *$10,000.*

§ 170. In reporting sermons place the figure for the Book or Epistle in the *first* position, for the chapter in the *second* position and for the verse in the *third* position. This rule may be applied when reference is made to any volume of a work when the number of the volume, chapter, and section or page is given.

POSITIVE AND NEGATIVE WORDS.

§ 171. Positive and negative words that begin with *il, im, in, ir,* should be distinguished by doubling the first consonant; words in *ir* being written according to the rules of the upward and downward r; thus, L^3:G*l, legal,* L^3:L:G*l, illegal,* Mtr:L^3, *material,* M: Mtr:L^3, *immaterial,* R^{1}shn:L, *rational,* R^1:Rshn:L, *irrational,* R^2:sLt, *resolute,* R^2s:Lt, *irresolute.* Write both the upward and downward r in the negative when the downward letter does not produce a good joining.

———

HOW TO ACQUIRE SPEED.

§ 172. When the student has written all the writing exercises, and also the reading exercises—first covering the key and then comparing what he has written with the engraved short-hand— and can write without hesitation any and all of the words given, he is ready for dictation practice. A good plan for the student is to take a series of graded readers and get some one to read to him, the person reading varying his speed to suit the writer's. When one of the lower readers is written through take the next highest, and so on until all have been written. The student should not try to write fast at first, but should endeavor to make his outlines correctly, or his notes will be illegible. If any difficulty is experienced in writing a word a circle should be made around it, and when the article is finished the words in rings should be written over and over, pronouncing the word each time, until it can be written without any hesitation. Everything written must be read, and it is excellent practice to read what was written a week or ten days before. If you have no series of readers take some easy article from a paper or book and write it several times, or if it does not become too irksome, until a speed of from fifty to seventy-five words a minute is attained; then take something else and repeat. This will give an extended vocabulary; the forms are memorized almost unconsciously and the ability to write them without hesitation whenever the words are spoken is acquired. Speed in short-hand depends upon the facility with which when a word is spoken its true outline is recognized, and this is only reached by becoming familiar with the words in common use by writing them again and again. When the student can write at the rate of fifty words a minute he should begin to take notes of lectures and sermons. At first, of course, the writer will be unable to keep up with the speaker. A few trials will, however, materially increase his speed. The object at first should not be to write as rapidly as possible but simply to take down as much of what is said as can be readily deciphered afterwards. The writer should not leave off in the middle of a sentence and commence another with the speaker, but should try to secure as many complete phrases and sentences as possible. These may be abbreviated, if necessary, in order to enable the writer to preserve the drift of the speaker's discourse. In this manner an intelligible transcript could be furnished. The writer should accustom himself to be several words behind the speaker, because in following rapid speakers if he has not trained himself in this particular he will find it extremely difficult to recover lost ground. As to the length of time necessary to acquire a speed of from 100 to 120 words a minute much depends of course, upon the natural ability of the writer and the amount of time he is willing to bestow daily upon the task.

§ 173. Beginners are apt to lose much time in turning over the leaves of their reporting books. The following plan, recommended by Mr. Thos. A. Reed, the leading English reporter, is perhaps the best that can be adopted: "While writing on the upper half of the leaf introduce the second finger of the left hand between it and the next leaf, keeping the leaf on which you are writing steady by the first finger and thumb. While writing on the lower part of the page shift the leaf by degrees, till it is about half way up the book; when it is convenient, lift up the thumb and the leaf will turn over almost by itself. This is the best plan for writing on a desk or table. When writing on the knee the first finger should be introduced instead of the second, and the leaf be shifted up only about two inches. The finger should be introduced at the first pause the speaker makes, or at any other convenient opportunity that presents itself." The writer should confine himself to one side of the book till it is filled in this way, and then turn it over, begin at the end and write in the same manner on the blank pages.

THE AMANUENSIS.

When the student can for several minutes maintain an average speed of about one hundred words a minute, and legibly transcribe his notes, he is ready, so far as short-hand is concerned, to accept a position as amanuensis. But other qualifications besides ability to write and read short-hand are necessary, and, in fact, indispensable.

A good style of penmanship, not an ornate, flourishing hand, but a plain, readable, rapid style is important. Ability to operate a writing machine with accuracy and at a fair rate of speed is also necessary.

Good spelling and capitalization are of course requisite, for inaccuracies which might escape the glance of the hurried reader of a pen written sheet are very conspicuous when printed.

The amanuensis should understand punctuation; but if he does not, he must become familiar with it, by studying some good text book on the subject, and also noting the marks used in correctly written letters or other articles. Avoid using too many punctuation marks.

The mere ability to put down in legible short-hand and accurately transcribe what is dictated is not the whole duty of the amanuensis. He should be able to write a good business-like letter himself, and be acquainted with common business terms; he should also have a thorough knowledge of grammar and composition, so as to be able to reconstruct a sentence dictated in ambiguous language.

The amanuensis should attend strictly to business. He should confine his thoughts to his work; listen attentively to what is being dictated and try to comprehend it, so if it becomes necessary to refer back to any part it can be found without delay.

If at any time the amanuensis does not clearly understand what is said he should ask the person dictating to repeat. He should not trust to luck or inspiration to supply it when transcribing his notes; it is better to acknowledge his inability to keep up rather than to give the impression that he is getting every word, and then be compelled to hand in an incorrect transcript.

An amanuensis will have to become familiar with the ways and business of his employer before he can do his work satisfactorily. Every business has peculiar terms, names and expressions which the amanuensis must learn. A good way to do this is to take the firm's catalogue, circulars, etc., and write and re-write, in short-hand, the technical terms until memorized. The student, when practicing for speed, should get all the business catalogues and circulars possible and write the technical terms and names of articles handled, until conversant with their outlines.

Be neat, both in personal appearance and work. A letter with marks of erasure scattered through it looks slovenly, unattractive and has less weight than a neatly written one.

Be polite. Many an amanuensis has lost his position from a lack of proper courtesy and respect.

To be successful, the amanuensis must work to his employer's interest. He should exercise great care in transcribing his letters and get them out as rapidly as possible. It may be necessary at times to remain later than usual, but the amanuensis should not complain or act disagreeable, as in all probability the extra work will not be forgotten.

The position of the amanuensis is one of trust and responsibility, and no business or professional man would care to employ one in whom he could not place the utmost confidence. He must possess a good moral character and hold strictly inviolate all knowledge of his employer's affairs, or he will not long retain a position where business privacies must be strictly regarded.

In conclusion, the amanuensis must not be content to *just* hold his place, he should endeavor to rise in his business as well as in the estimation of his employer, and strive by every honorable means to reach such a stage that he is almost indispensable. To do this he must work hard to obtain a correct knowledge of the business, be faithful, honest and upright, willing, but not officious.

HINTS ON REPORTING.

If there is any doubt about the proper word being written a circle should be placed around the outline or a cross under it. If a word has been lost to the ear a caret should be made under the line to denote the omission. If part of a sentence should be thus lost, the same mark may be made and a space left proportionated to the number of words omitted. The letters *nh* (not heard) in long-hand may mean that to the extent of a sentence or more the speaker was not audible to the reporter. The advantage derived in thus noting these omissions is that if the speech was taken for a newspaper the omissions may be commented on as [here the speaker's voice was so low as to be inaudible], etc.

A large X in the left hand margin may be used to denote an error on the part of the speaker on which it may be necessary to comment when transcribing.

In reporting a sermon, a quotation from the Scripture or the text, etc., need not be written in full; the commencing and concluding words with a long dash between is sufficient.

In reporting a speech the outbursts of the audience should be recorded at the very point where such occur; all remarks by the auditors should be noted both in the notes and the transcript. In describing the kind of applause, laughter, etc., the adjective should be written *last*. Thus, what the reporter would describe in his transcript as "loud and continued applause" should be written in the notes P¹⅃s L¹:D T³:N:D, for he will not know that it is continued until it has lasted some time.

When a phrase is repeated several times in a sentence, a waved dash line may be used to denote the repeated words instead of writing them every time they occur.

In reporting lectures or speeches on special topics, wherein a term or phrase may be expected to occur frequently, the phonographer will find it advisable to prepare contractions for the occasion, or extemporize them when reporting.

LEGAL REPORTING.

For reporting the examination of witnesses, the note book should have a line running down the left hand side of the page about an inch from the margin. All questions should begin close to the left side of the page, and if occupying more than a line each subsequent line should begin as the first. The full answer should be written at the right of the ruled line. This plan is very convenient for reference. The reporter should be provided with a seat at a table or desk, so placed, if possible, that he shall face the witness stand and be near to it, and at the same time so situated that he can hear whatever may be said by the presiding judge or by the counsel. .

At the top of the first page of the notes write the name of the court, where held, term, name of the presiding judge or judges, the title of the cause, its number and character, the names of the counsel appearing for each party, and lastly the date of the commencement of the trial.

In criminal cases the examination of jurors previous to being sworn should be reported, as exceptions to the rulings of the court in regard to their competency may be taken. The opening statement of the counsel for the plaintiff should be reported, but the remarks of counsel need not be taken down unless specially requested. The judges charge unless read from manuscript, must always be reported. Motions and objections of counsel, and rulings of the court need not be reported in full, a synopsis being all that is necessary.

All testimony must be taken down with literal exactness, and in the transcript the language of the witness, no matter how ungrammatical should be left unchanged. Notice all mispronunciations, wherever possible. Write K^1*nt* for *can't*, K^1:N*t*, *cannot*, K^3*nt*, *couldn't*, K^3*d*:N*t*, *could not*, D^2*nt*, *don't*, D^2 N^1*t*, *do not*, D^3*nt*, *didn't*, D^3 N^1*t*, *did not*. *Would not* and *wouldn't*, *won't* and *will not*, and similar words should be so written that in transcribing the notes the exact language of the witness may be given.

The name of each witness should form a fresh heading and be written in long hand. The name of the examiner may be written in phonography, and should be placed under that of the witness If the judge or other person interferes and asks a question, the name of the interrupting party should precede the question. If he asks several questions, his name need not be repeated after the first, but care must be taken to insert the name of the original examiner when he resumes. When a document is put in, note the fact, and if it is read, record this also.

Transcripts of legal proceedings should be written on legal cap, both sides of the paper, and the first page should be used as the title page of each day's report. Each title page, like the first page of the notes, should contain the name of the court, title of cause, judge's name, names of counsel, plaintiff and defendant, and date of trial.

REPORTING FOR THE PRESS.

The necessary qualifications for a successful reporter are a good natural ability, a good education, the power of expressing his thoughts in clear, concise and unambiguous manner; ability to condense (or "boil down" as it is called) or to expand when necessary; ability to distinguish between a good and a poor item and to "write up" the good one in an attractive way. A knowledge of Phonography is not absolutely necessary, yet it will prove a valuable aid to the reporter when his "assignment" consists of an interview, lecture, or sermon, even when only a synopsis is required.

Interviewing is one of the most difficult branches of reportorial work. It requires special tact and discrimination, self-possession, easy, fluent, conversational powers, and ability to obtain the desired information even when the party interviewed is determined not to divulge it, and to escape the humiliation of becoming the interviewed instead of the interviewer. In case the party interviewed is some prominent person from some other city or country, his personal appearance should first be described and then the interview, if the man's prominence and the subject warrant it, may follow in full; but if the person is not very prominent, nor the subject one of special interest, a brief synopsis only should be given. After the novice has several times had a voluminous unimportant article handed by the "city editor" to some experienced reporter with instructions to "cut that down to six lines," he will learn to be more discriminating or else seek some other branch of the profession.

In reporting a lecture, political meeting, etc., the reporter should, in the beginning of his article, mention the size and appearance of the audience, decorations of hall if any, names of gentlemen seated on the platform and anything of interest occurring prior to the opening of the exercises. All preliminary remarks should be noted. If the speaker is introduced to the audience by the chairman or any other person, it should be noticed about as follows: "The chairman (or name of party introducing) then introduced the Hon. Peter Cooper, who spoke substantially as follows:" then give the speech, noting all interruptions of any kind. In transcribing the notes the various interruptions should be inclosed in brackets; thus, [A voice: "That's so."] [Laughter.]

In conclusion, whether reporting every word, or simply preparing condensed reports of long harrangues containing but few principles, the reporter is called upon to exercise his mental powers to a great extent. A man may make an indifferent speech so far as language is concerned, but overflowing with excellent thoughts or valuable information, which it is the duty of the reporter to condense, improve, and, in fact, render intelligible. In short, it is expected of the reporter that he will make a good speech for a bad speaker.

WORDS WITH L OR R HOOKS.

The following list contains nearly all the words in common use with a distinct vowel sound preceding the *l* or *r* where the *l* or *r* is expressed by the hook instead of stem. A general rule followed in the formation of this list is that when *r* is immtdiately followed by *m*, or by *f* immediately followed by another consonant, the hook is used. When *m* and *r*, *n* and *r*, or *ch* and *r*, are the only consonants in a word, unless two vowels intervene or there is a final vowel sound then express the *r* by the hook. D and *r* with an intervening *third-place* vowel sound may be expressed by Dr. When *r* and *l* are the first or only consonants in a word they should be expressed by *Rl*.

LIST.

Accord, K₁rd
accordingly, K₁rd:NGl
accordance, K₁rd:Ns
accordant, K₁rd:Nt
accordian. Kr:D₁n
adverse, D¹:Vrs
adversity, D²:Vrs:T
apartment, P¹rt:Mnt
attorney, T²r:N
Bold, B₂ld
boldly, B₂ld:L
burglar, B³r:Gl:R
Calcinate, K¹l:sNt
calcine, K₁l:sN
call, K₁l
carbon, Kr:B¹n
care, K²r
cared, K²rd
carmine, K¹r:Mn
carnage, K₁r:N:J
carnal, K¹r:Nl
carnation, K³r:Nshn
carpet, Kr:P¹t
cartoon, K¹r:Tn
chair, CH²r
character, K⁴r:Ktr

Charles, CH¹r:Ls
charm, CH¹r:M
cheer, CH³r
cheerful, CH³r:Fl
child, CH¹ld
children, CH³l:Drn
coarse, K²rs
coarsely, K²r:sL
coarseness, K⁴rs:Ns
cold, K²ld
coldness. K²ld:Ns
collect, Kl:K:T²
collection, K²l:Kshn
college, Kl:J¹
colonial, Kl:N:L²
colonize, K¹l:Ns
colony, K¹l:N
comfortless, .F²rt:Ls
comparative, .P¹rt:V
convert, .V²₁t
converse, .V²rs
cordage, Krd:J¹
corner, K¹r:Nr
cornet, K²r:Nt
cornice, K¹r:Ns
coronation, K²r:Nshn

corporal, Kr:P¹r:L
corporeal, Kr:P²r:L
correct, Kr:K:T²
corrupt, Kr:P²t
cortical, K¹rt:Kl
courage. Kr:J²
course, K²rs
court, K²rt
courteous, Kr:T²s
courtier, Krt:R²
create, Kr:T³
culminate, Kl:M:N:T₂
culmination, K²l:M:Nshn
cupboard, K:P²:Brd
cur, K²r
curdle, K²rd:L
curse, K²rs
cursed, K²rst
cursory, K²r:sR
curtain, K²rt:N
curtail, K²rt:L
Dark, D¹r:K
dear, D³r
dearer, D³r:R
dearness, D³r:Ns
debark, D¹:Br:K
department, D¹:Prt:Mnt
deportment, D²:Prt:Mnt
dirk, D²r:K
during, D³r
Effulgent, F²l:Jnt
eternity, T²r:N:T
Ferment, F²r:Mnt
fertilize, F²rt:Ls
farther, F¹tr
firkin, F²r:Kn
for, F¹r
former, F¹r:Mr
fulgent, F²l:Jnt
furlough, F²r:L
furnace, F²r:Ns
furnish, F²rn:SH
furniture, F²rn:T:R
further, F²rtr
furthest, F²r:THst
Garb, Gr:B¹
garden, G¹rd:N
gargle, G¹r:Gl
garment, G¹r:Mnt
garner, G¹r:Nr
garnish, Grn:SH¹
garter, G¹tr

germ, J²r:M
germane, J²r:Mn
Germany, J²r:M:N
girded, G²rd:D
gold, G²ld
griddle, G²rd:L
guard, G¹rd
guardian, G¹rd:N
guerdon, G²rd:N
gurgle, G²r:Gl
Ignore, G₂:Nr
ignorance, G³:Nrns
incarnate, N¹:Kr:Nt
Jerk, J²r:K
journey, J²r:N
Merely, Mr:L³
moral, Mr:L₁
morally, Mr:L¹
more, M²r
Mormon, M¹r:Mn
murder, M²rdr
myrtle, Mrt:l₂
Narrate, Nr:T₂
narrative, Nr:T¹v
near, N²r
nearly, N²r:L
nor, N¹r
nurse, N²rs
nurture, N²r:Tr
Occur, K²r
occurrent, K²r:Nt
operate, P¹rt
operator, P¹rtr
operation, P²rshn
Parallel, P₁r:L:L
paramount, P¹r:Mnt
parcel, P¹rs:L
parsley, P¹r:sL
partake, P²rt:K
perceive, P³rs:V
perception, P²rs:Pshn
percussion, P²r:Kshn
peremptory, P²r:MP:Tr
perfect, P²rf:Kt
perfection, P²rf:Kshn
perfume, P²r:F:M
perhaps, P¹r:Ps
perjure, P²r:Jr
perjury, P²r:Jr
permanent, P²r:Mn:Nt
permeate, P²r:M:T
permission, P²r:Mshn

permit, P³ᵣ:Mt
persist, Pʳss:T
perspire, Pᵢrs:P:R
pervade, P²r:Vd
perverse, P²r:Vᵣs
pyramid, P³r:Md
political, P³lt:Kl
politics, P¹lt:Ks
portray, Pᵣr:Tr
Rail, Rᵢl
raillery, Rᵢl:R
real, R³l
realize, Rᵢls
realized, R¹lst
reality, R¹l:T
record, R⁴:Krd
recur, R²:Kr
regard, R¹:Grd
relentless, Rₑl:Nt:Ls
relevance, Rᵢl:Vns
relief, R³lf
relished, Rᵢl:SHt
roll, Rᵢl
roller, R²l:R
rollic, R¹l:K
rule, R³l
ruling, R³l:NG
ruler, R³l:R
rural, R³:Rl
Separate, sP₂r:T
separation, sP²rshn
shark, SH¹r:K
shirk, SH r:K
short, SHᵢrt
speculate, sP₇:Klt
speculation, sP⁴:Klshn

spirit, sP₃rt
sure, SHₐr
Telegraph, T₂l:Grf
telegraphy, T³l:Gr:F
tell, T³l
term, T²r:M
terminate, Tᵣr:M:N:T
terminus, T²r:M:Ns
their, DHₐr
there, DHₐr
third, THₐrd
thirst, THᵣrst
thirty, THₐr:T
Thursday, THₐrs:D
till, T₃l
told, T₂ld
torment, Tᵢr:Mnt
toward, T²rd
turgid, T₂r:Jd
turkey, Tᵣr:K
turmoil, T²r:M:L
Verbal, Vᵣr:Bl
verdict, V⁴ₐd:Kt
verse, V₂rs
version, V²rshn
vertebra, V₂rt:Br
vertex, V₂rt:Ks
vertical, V²rt:Kl
virgo, V₇r:G
virtual, Vᵣrt:L
virtue, Vᵣrt
virulence. V²r:Lns
virulent. V₂r:Lnt
vortex, V¹rt:Ks
vulgar, V₂l:Gr
vulgarity, V²l:Gr:T

INDEX.

SHN AND TER HOOKS.

LENGTHENING.

HALVING.

CONTRACTIONS.

PHRASE WRITING.

RULES FOR FORMING CONTRACTIONS.

www.ingramcontent.com/pod-product-compliance
Lightning Source LLC
Chambersburg PA
CBHW020306090426
42735CB00009B/1243